Dancing With Change

How To P.I.V.O.T.™ Through Life's Transitions - with Less Fear, More Agility and Greater Agency

By

Dr. Khutso Madubanya

Founder of Dance With Change™

For permission requests, write to **USA Writers and Publishers**

support@usawritersandpublishers.com
www.usawritersandpublishers.com

Paperback ISBN: 978-1-967086-53-5
Hard Cover ISBN: 978-1-967086-54-2
Printed and published in the United States of America.

DEDICATION

For change—
not as an enemy to defeat,
but as a partner
we are learning to dance with.

WHAT PEOPLE SAY AFTER WE DANCE WITH CHANGE

"I cried. Eye-opening. Engaging."
— **Areion Thomas, Educator**

"Dr. Khutso's positivity is contagious. Learning about the P.I.V.O.T.™ Method gave me language — and permission — to approach change differently."
— **MQ, President, Women's Business Network**

"The P.I.V.O.T.™ Method broke change down in a way that finally made it feel possible — and even hopeful."
— **AB, Preschool Teacher**

"The learnings and insight behind P.I.V.O.T.™ — oh wow. It shifted my thinking, and I'll be using it every day."
— **Nicky VR, Financial Advisor**

*"P.I.V.O.T.™ helped me realize that change can be good —
regardless of how uncomfortable it feels. Going back to who you used
to be is harder than moving forward into who you're becoming. You
don't live there anymore. And always remember to breathe."*
— Antoinette W., Educator

*"Dr. Khutso is positive, grounded, and incredibly strong... I will
always remember to P.I.V.O.T.™ and dance my way through
change."*
— Isabella W., Western Michigan University Student

"Dr. Khutso left us with a tool we will carry for the rest of our lives."
— Ella W, Western Michigan University

AUTHOR'S NOTE

This book was not written to be rushed.

Dancing With Change is an invitation to meet life's transitions with greater steadiness, self-trust, and grace. You don't need to read it from beginning to end in one sitting, and you don't need to "get it right." You may find yourself drawn to certain chapters more than others, depending on the season of change you're in. That's intentional.

This work builds upon the inner reckoning I began in *No More Free Passes*—a call to stop proving and start becoming. While book named the cost of extreme independence, Dancing With Change™, offers a way to move beyond it, and beyond other transitions that quietly ask us to redefine who we are.

At the heart of this book is The P.I.V.O.T.™ Method—a framework designed not as a checklist for action, but as a mental recalibration tool. It helps stabilize the mind during transitions, preventing fear from taking over and allowing adaptability to emerge naturally.

This book is for people navigating change in both personal and professional spaces. Its principles apply at the individual level and extend into collective life across teams, classrooms, and organizations shaped by leaders and educators.

I intend for this work to support personal growth while also contributing to environments where people can learn, adapt, and grow without fear, pressure, or the need to perform.

My wish is that the principles in this book become a companion for you during moments of uncertainty. A reminder that you already have what you need.

Change will keep coming.
But so will you.

Feeling off-balance during unexpected change?

Download your **FREE 1-page**

P.I.V.O.T.™ Guide — a short, calming reset to help you steady your mind and prevent fear from taking over at:

Note on the Word Pivot

The word "pivot" has become widely used in leadership, entrepreneurship, and coaching, and several authors have created their own PIVOT or P.I.V.O.T. acronyms. The P.I.V.O.T.™ Method in this book is my original framework for mental recalibration in moments of change. Here, P.I.V.O.T. stands for Pause, Introspect, Vector, Overcome, and Travel Forward — five inner mindset shifts that move us from resistance to flow, from proving to being. This method is part of the broader Dance With Change™ philosophy and reflects my personal journey, research, and lived experience across continents and seasons of transformation.

Table of Contents

PRELUDE – AN INVITATION TO THE DANCE

Change rarely asks for permission.
It arrives unannounced — and often unwanted.

When change comes without warning or identity, we resist not because change itself is dangerous, but because it disrupts our sense of meaning. It interrupts the stories we tell ourselves about who we are and where we're going.

For a long time, I believed strength meant holding everything together when change tried to pull it apart. I believed resilience meant pushing harder and staying in control. That belief carried me across continents, careers, and identities. It helped me survive — and even succeed.

But it didn't help when my life stopped making sense.

When that happened, trying harder wasn't the answer. Neither was control. What helped was slowing down long enough to notice what was actually happening and how I was responding. That's when my relationship with change began to shift.

Dance With Change™ is not about fixing problems or forcing things to work out. It's about learning how to stay steady on the inside when life changes, so fear doesn't take over before you've had a chance to think and respond.

I developed the *P.I.V.O.T.*™ *Method* to help you stop fighting change and start moving with it. It's not a set of extra steps to add to your already full day. It's a way to steady your thinking when you feel unsure of yourself, lose confidence, or don't know what to do next.

Whether your life is shifting quietly or being turned upside down, this book begins with a simple reminder: you already have what you need to get through change. What we often lose in difficult moments is access to that inner strength, especially when we're under pressure.

So, pause for a moment.
Let go of the idea that you must power through change flawlessly or have everything figured out.

This book is an invitation — not to control change, but to meet it with steadiness, self-trust, and agency.

Take a breath.
Let's begin.

WHY THE DANCE?

When people hear *Dance With Change*, they often ask, *Are you a dancer? Do you teach dance?* I usually smile and say, *No. I love to dance, but I teach change.*

This almost always elicits a pause.

Dance is a metaphor I chose to suggest ease, agility, and responsiveness — the opposite of gripping life with force and rigidity. Change is inevitable, but how we respond to it determines how we move through it and how we emerge on the other side. Most people adapt eventually, but some do so with far less fear and overwhelm. The dance metaphor helps make that distinction.

Dancing is not about control.
It is about relationship.

In any dance, there is rhythm, movement, and connection. You don't dominate the music. You listen to it. You adjust your weight, timing, and posture. When the tempo shifts, you don't argue with it. You move with it.

Most of us are taught to take charge of our lives. We plan the steps, set the pace, and rely on discipline to keep things predictable until life changes the rhythm without asking us.

In those moments, life takes the lead, not us. We suffer not because the movement is wrong, but because we are off beat, trying to dance a waltz while life is playing a tango. We tighten, brace, and push harder, hoping the old rhythm will return.

But in dance, resistance creates strain. Rigidity leads to missteps. The more you fight the movement, the more exhausting it becomes.

Dancing With Change is an invitation to stop bracing against the movement beneath your life and learn how to stay balanced within it. Change may not be kind, but you deserve to move through it with less fear, more agency, and deeper self-trust.

PART I:
THE PRINCIPLES

Chapter 1 – The Paradox of Change: Losing Control to Gain it Back

It is October 26, 2021, and once again, I am starting over in another country.

I have lost count of how many times I have done this — eight countries and countless reinventions later. But this time is different. This time, I am not alone. I am immigrating with my children.

For over three decades before motherhood, I moved freely and fearlessly across the world. Now, as the solo parent of three, I was carrying more than luggage. I was carrying grief — fresh from an unexpected breakup with my last husband — and the quiet responsibility of helping my children say goodbye to the only father figure they had ever known.

Saying goodbye to family at the Johannesburg airport felt surreal. Sad, yes — but mostly hopeful. The excitement of a new beginning softened the pain that still throbbed beneath the surface.

Nothing about that moment at the airport had prepared me for the years of tsunamis that followed.

Within months of arriving in the United States, everything began to unravel. I found myself engulfed in a tsunami - unexpectedly unemployed, entangled in a grueling legal battle, completing doctoral studies, and making an involuntary career pivot, all while trying to help my children adjust to losing the only father-figure they had ever known and living in a foreign country without a support system.

The tsunami taught me something I had never fully understood before: pushing against what you cannot control only makes adaptation harder. Change is inevitable. Resistance is human — but it comes at a cost. We may not choose resistance when it appears, but we can choose whether to remain in it.

When life strips away certainty, support, and familiar structure all at once, the mind searches desperately for footing. It reaches for control, not because we are weak, but because we are trying to find meaning again.

The harder I tried to regain control, the more overwhelmed I became. What I thought was strength — pushing harder, holding it together, proving resilience — was quietly working against me. Change did not destabilize me because I was incapable of it. It destabilized me by disrupting my sense of direction, identity, and meaning.

When that inner orientation shifts, fear often rushes in to fill the space. Resistance follows as the mind's attempt to steady itself when its internal compass begins to spin.

This is the *paradox* we rarely name.

We talk about change as something to manage or conquer. We label people as adaptable or resistant, strong or fragile. Yet resistance is often simply the moment when change arrives faster than our ability to make sense of it.

Your story may look very different from mine. Your change may be quieter, slower, or less visible from the outside. But when change disrupts familiarity or identity, whether in small ways or seismic ones, the internal experience often feels the same:

Disorientation.
Fear.
A tightening of control.
A pull to resist.

Not because something is wrong with us.
But because the mind is trying to regain balance.

My promise to you is not that change will be painless.

It does not have to be *punishing*.

Whenever change disrupts your sense of direction, especially when it arrives unexpectedly, there is another way to meet it, without fighting yourself with force, perfection, or certainty.

This book is an invitation to explore that way.

If you have ever felt unsteady, resistant, or afraid in the face of change, this book is for you.

If you're willing, take my hand.

Let's begin.

Chapter 2 – When Change Forces You to Choose What You Don't Want

It was the middle of May 2022 when I finally thought I'd caught a break.

After what felt like a million multi-step job interviews, I walked into a Zoom interview room and knew instantly that this time was different. Unlike all the others, this conversation had ease to it. In fact, I didn't even think I wanted the job — my eyes were set on something else. I remember closing my laptop and thinking, "I don't really want this job, but I have a feeling they're going to offer it to me."

I had been unemployed for several months, having lost my job soon after arriving in the United States. For the first time in my life, I was on government assistance. The Medicaid and food stamps I relied on were barely enough to feed my three children. I had no backup plan, no safety net. The modest savings I had brought with me from Africa were disappearing fast.

I didn't need the perfect job. I needed **a** job.

So, when the offer came a few days later, I accepted it immediately.

I was grateful for the speed. After months of waiting and rejection, momentum felt like relief. The salary wasn't what I had hoped for, but the role sounded close enough to what I knew: digital marketing, media, campaigns.

I had run my own digital marketing agency for a few years before that. I thought I understood campaigns.

I was wrong.

Within days, it became clear that what I thought this job involved bore little resemblance to the reality. My new supervisor might as well have been speaking Greek. Every industry has its own language, and although he used familiar words — digital, media, campaign — they carried entirely different meanings in this context. I felt instantly out of my depth.

The manager who hired me, who would resign just a week into my training, was patient and reassuring. He was confident I was the right hire. After all, I had run my own agency.

I wasn't so sure.

On his last day, desperate for reassurance, I joked, "If I could give birth to three children, I'd be okay with this job, right?"

He smiled. "Whatever makes you feel empowered, Khutso."

That was the beginning of an unexpected career pivot — learning a new role on the fly. After he left, it was just one colleague and me, and technically, I was the senior.

I needed the job.
But I didn't love the job.

At one point, I admitted to HR and my new manager, "I think I made a mistake. This job isn't what I thought it would be."

My new manager was kind and optimistic. He believed my experience would transfer quickly. But I wasn't convinced — and part of me wasn't sure I even wanted it to.

Within weeks, he gave me a harsh but fair ultimatum. "I'll give you three months to find another position," he said. "I'll support you however I can. But after that, I'll need to fill this role. It's just not a good fit."

He was right. It wasn't a good fit.

But I couldn't afford to be unemployed again — not with three children in a new country and no support system. I didn't know how long another job search would take. I couldn't risk it.

I sat with the decision for days. In the end, I chose a third option: I would quietly look for other opportunities while doing everything I could to become indispensable where I was.

If I had to leave, it would be on my own terms.

The weeks that followed were bewildering. I felt everything at once: relief at being employed, humiliation at not knowing how to do basic tasks, shock at how unfamiliar this world was, guilt for taking a role that might have suited someone else better, and embarrassment at making rookie mistakes under managers young enough to be my children.

Eventually, I realized I had a choice.

I could either stay stuck, resisting my situation, or find a way to move with it.

That realization came to me at three o'clock one morning, lying awake while my thoughts spiraled. They jumped from court dates to school needs, from bills to deadlines, from exhaustion to fear. The job demanded more from me than I felt ready to give.

Somewhere between fatigue and surrender, I saw the pattern clearly.

I could keep fighting — proving myself, rushing to keep up, pushing against authority, trying to protect an identity that no longer fit.

Or I could stop resisting.

I could humble myself. I could slow down. I could focus on learning instead of proving. I could detach my sense of worth from the role I had been forced into.

I chose the second path.

The next morning, the relief was subtle but real. I wasn't suddenly confident, but I was no longer panicked about work. I felt steadier. More present.

What I didn't realize then was that this small internal shift, choosing to stop fighting and start listening, would quietly change how I moved through uncertainty.

I didn't have language for it yet.

But something important had begun.

I had just begun to move with my chaos instead of fighting it.

Chapter 3 – The Myths of Change: What Keeps Us from Dancing

Before we can learn to dance with change, we need to understand why change, unexpected change, so often feels threatening in the first place.

Much of what we call "fear of change" is not fear at all. It is disorientation — the loss of internal footing that occurs when meaning, identity, or expectations are disrupted. The myths we carry about change do not create this disruption; they give us the wrong explanations for it. When we misunderstand what is happening inside us, we move against it instead of with it.

Most of us internalize these myths early. They become a quiet background, shaping how we respond when life shifts unexpectedly. They keep us bracing instead of moving.

Here are five myths about change, and the truths that allow us to dance again.

Myth #1: Discomfort Means Something Is Wrong

Change does disrupt life as we know it. It alters routines, roles, expectations, and familiar reference points. That disruption is real, and it often feels chaotic from the inside.

The myth is not that change causes disruption.
The myth is that the discomfort we feel during disruption means something has gone wrong.

When change arrives unexpectedly, the mind loses its usual anchors. Meaning collapses before a new pattern has time to form. In that gap, the internal experience can feel noisy, unstable, even overwhelming. We label that experience "chaos" and assume it signals danger.

But chaos is not evidence that change is harmful.
It is evidence that the mind is still orienting.

Neuroscience shows that uncertainty activates the same brain regions associated with physical pain. No wonder the early moments of change feel uncomfortable. That discomfort does not signal disorder; it signals recalibration — the brain gathering information, testing assumptions, and searching for a new rhythm.

What we experience as chaos is often simply a transition without context.

Once meaning begins to reassemble, the noise quiets. Patterns emerge. What felt like disorder reveals its underlying structure as orientation returns.

When we stop treating discomfort as a warning sign and start recognizing it as a cue to slow down, to listen, to reorient, we regain our footing. The rhythm was always there. We couldn't hear it yet.

Myth #2: If You're Strong, Change Shouldn't Feel So Hard

We live in a culture that glorifies composure. We are praised for staying calm, holding it together, and pushing through even when circumstances are changing beneath our feet.

Over time, many of us internalize the idea that strength means stability. If we are capable, experienced, or resilient enough, we assume change should feel manageable — even seamless.

So, when change feels heavy, destabilizing, or emotionally taxing, we interpret that discomfort as a personal shortcoming. We wonder why we are struggling at all.

But struggle is not a sign of weakness. It is a sign that new demands are being processed.

When roles, expectations, or environments shift, the mind and body must recalibrate. Old reference points no longer apply, and new ones have not yet formed. That interim period often feels effortful, not because we lack strength, but because adaptation is underway.

Psychologists describe this capacity as emotional agility: the ability to experience uncertainty without becoming stuck in it. Research shows that people who allow themselves to feel discomfort rather than suppress it adapt more effectively over time.

Rigidity appears strong from the outside, but it limits movement. Flexibility restores balance. The moment we stop expecting change to feel easy, we stop interpreting effort as failure and begin to regain our rhythm.

Myth #3: You Need to Be Ready Before You Begin Change

"I'll change when I'm ready."
We tell ourselves this to feel safe. It creates the comforting illusion that clarity must come before action.

But readiness rarely precedes movement. It emerges through it.

What most of us are waiting for is not certainty. We are waiting for orientation. We want the mind to feel settled, the path to feel familiar, and the risk to feel contained. Until that happens, we hesitate, believing we are being prudent when we are often just stalled.

Readiness does not mean knowing what will happen next. It means regaining enough internal steadiness to take the next step without panic.

Behavioral science shows that confidence follows competence, not the other way around. Each small action helps the brain update its expectations, gradually replacing threat with familiarity. Movement creates information. Information restores orientation.

When we wait to feel ready, we often wait longer than necessary. When we move gently but intentionally, readiness begins to assemble around us.

Dancing with change does not require perfect timing or full clarity. It requires trusting that you can learn the steps as you go — once your footing has been steadied.

Myth #4: Control Means Safety

Control can feel comforting. We plan, organize, and manage to prevent surprises. For a long time, I believed that if I could control every variable, I could stay safe.

But control is often the mind's substitute for lost meaning. Psychologists call this the illusion of control: the belief that managing outcomes will eliminate uncertainty. It may soothe anxiety temporarily, but it often increases resistance over time.

When life requires improvisation, control becomes a source of tension. Tension disrupts rhythm. True safety does not come from certainty; it comes from centeredness — from knowing who you are even when outcomes remain unclear.

You cannot hold the music still, but you can find your rhythm within it.

Myth #5: Change Means Losing Who You Are

This myth is subtle and deeply human. We fear that if we adapt too much, we will lose ourselves.

But what we fear losing is not identity itself — it is *coherence*. It is the story that helps us recognize ourselves across change. When that story fractures, it can feel like disappearance.

Change does not erase identity; it refines it. Each transition carries forward what has been learned, tested, and strengthened. Neuroscience calls this neuroplasticity — the brain's ability to reorganize through experience.

Dancing with change does not strip us of who we are. It helps us see that identity is not lost in transition — it evolves while remaining recognizably ours.

These myths shape how many of us interpret the internal experience of change. They don't arise because change is inherently threatening, but because disruption unsettles meaning before new reference points have time to form.

When we misread discomfort as danger, effort as failure, or uncertainty as a signal to stop, we respond to change in ways that add strain rather than restore footing.

Before exploring how to move through change differently, it helps to be clear about what kind of change we are actually addressing and who this approach is meant to support.

That is where we turn next.

Chapter 4 – What Kind of Change This Book Addresses

Before we move forward, we need to pause and clarify what we mean by "change," because not all change asks the same thing of us.

Some change is chosen. We plan it, pursue it, and often welcome the growth it promises. We decide to take a new job, receive a scholarship, begin a relationship, or step into something meaningful but uncertain. Even when it feels uncomfortable, chosen change usually carries a sense of agency. We may feel nervous, but we remain oriented. We feel in charge of the movement.

This book is **not** primarily about that kind of change.

This book speaks to unexpected, destabilizing change — the kind that arrives without warning and disrupts our sense of meaning, identity, or direction. It does not simply alter circumstances; it unsettles the internal story we rely on to understand who we are and how life is supposed to work.

This kind of disruption can emerge in personal or professional life. A relationship dissolves. Someone we love dies. A job ends unexpectedly. A career shifts overnight. New technologies reshape roles and expectations. When the internal story fractures, the mind loses its footing.

This is the moment *Dancing With Change*™ speaks to.

For some people, disruption shows up as fear, overwhelm, or a feeling of freezing. For others, it appears as withdrawal, self-doubt, or a sudden loss of confidence. Still others respond by over-functioning — pushing harder, tightening control, or trying to prove their worth through relentless effort.

These reactions are often misread as personality traits or character flaws.

They are not.

They are signals that meaning has been disrupted.

When orientation shifts, the mind instinctively seeks stability before it allows movement. Fear is not the problem; it is a byproduct of disorientation. Resistance is not defiance; it is an attempt to regain balance when internal bearings have been shaken.

This is why people experience change differently.

Some adapt quickly, even under pressure. Others move more slowly or cautiously. The difference is rarely intelligence or resilience. It is the speed at which meaning can be reconstructed after disruption.

Many people who describe themselves as "afraid of change" are not afraid of change itself. They are afraid of what change has historically cost them — safety, belonging, stability, identity, or control. Their nervous systems have learned that change often comes at a cost.

This book is especially for them.

It is also for people who generally welcome change until a particular disruption catches them off guard. In those moments, before their systems know how to respond, this book offers a way to regain internal footing and adapt consciously.

And it is for those who fall somewhere in between — people who want to move forward yet feel unsettled, who sense they should be "handling this better," but cannot quite find their balance.

Beyond the personal level, this work also applies within organizations. Leaders, educators, and professionals often ask why people resist change. Yet you cannot guide others through what you do not first understand within yourself. By reframing resistance as disrupted sensemaking, this book offers leaders a new lens — and practical mindset tools to strengthen a team's capacity to adapt.

What this book is not is equally important.

It is not a collection of quick fixes, productivity hacks, or forced positivity. It does not promise to eliminate fear, bypass discomfort, or accelerate adaptation through pressure. And it does not treat resistance as weakness or something to be corrected.

Sustainable movement does not come from force.

It comes from restored meaning.

This is where The P.I.V.O.T.™ Method comes in.

P.I.V.O.T.™ is not a behavioral checklist or performance system. It is a mental recalibration process — a way of restoring inner orientation when change disrupts sensemaking.

I developed this during the height of my own tsunami, when I had no backup plan, no safety net, and no clear map forward. The only tool I had was my mind. I learned that the conversations we have with ourselves shape how we move through uncertainty far more than the circumstances we face. P.I.V.O.T.™ emerged as a way to work with the mind when navigating difficult transitions – not before, not after, but *during* transition.

Now that we have named the kind of change we are dancing with, we can move deeper into P.I.V.O.T.™ — what it is, and how it can help you find steadiness within change.

Chapter 5 — The P.I.V.O.T.™ Framework

P.I.V.O.T.™ did not arrive as a polished idea or a neatly named framework. It emerged gradually, from inside a period of intense transition — the one I described earlier — when nearly every part of my life was shifting at once.

By the summer of 2022, my children and I had recently arrived in the United States. I was navigating legal uncertainty, financial strain, doctoral work, and a job I had accepted out of necessity rather than readiness. Externally, nothing felt settled. Internally, I was exhausted — not only by what was happening, but by how much energy I was spending fighting the reality I was in.

One night, sometime around three in the morning, I found myself awake again, replaying the same thoughts on a loop. They jumped from fear to self-doubt, from urgency to regret, from what I had lost to what I feared might come next. I had no tools at the time — only my mind, already stretched thin.

What became clear in that moment was not a solution, but a distinction.

Some of the conversations I was having with myself made the chaos harder to carry. Others, subtle as they were, seemed to steady me just enough to stay present. Even though nothing around me changed, certain thoughts grounded me, while others sent me spiraling.

That realization marked a turning point. I began paying closer attention — not to the change itself, but to where my mind got stuck while trying to move through it. Patterns started to surface. Panic about the unknown. Questions about identity. Overwhelmed when learning something new. Fear of mistakes, a constant pull toward what had been left behind.

I came to see these moments as *friction points* — places where resistance drained energy and made adaptation feel harder than it needed to be.

Over time, I began experimenting with how I responded internally at each point. Not by forcing confidence or rushing toward answers, but by gently guiding my attention, my self-talk, and my sense of direction while change was already in motion.

Those small internal adjustments did not remove uncertainty. But they did something more important: they helped me feel steady enough to stay engaged — to learn, to recover from mistakes, and to keep moving forward without collapsing or hardening.

What eventually took shape from those observations is the framework you'll explore in this chapter: **P.I.V.O.T.™** — a way of recalibrating the mind during active transition, when familiar anchors have loosened, and clarity has not yet arrived.

What P.I.V.O.T.™ Is — and What It Is Not

P.I.V.O.T.™ is not a productivity system, a checklist, or a set of behaviors to perform. It is not about fixing yourself or pushing harder to adapt faster.

P.I.V.O.T.™ works internally. It focuses on what happens in the mind when change disrupts your sense of direction, identity, or certainty. It helps you notice and gently guide the inner conversation that naturally begins when familiar ways of working or living fall away.

Most approaches to change focus on what people should do externally: learn new skills, follow new processes, adopt new strategies. They assume that once the right actions are identified, people will simply adapt.

But when change arrives, action is rarely the real problem.

The deeper challenge is what happens **inside**. When people feel disoriented, unsafe, or disconnected from themselves, even the best strategies struggle to take hold. Without internal grounding, adaptability becomes exhausting instead of sustainable.

P.I.V.O.T.™ begins there.

Each part of the framework speaks to a different friction point — a place where the mind tends to tighten, rush, or resist while change is already underway.

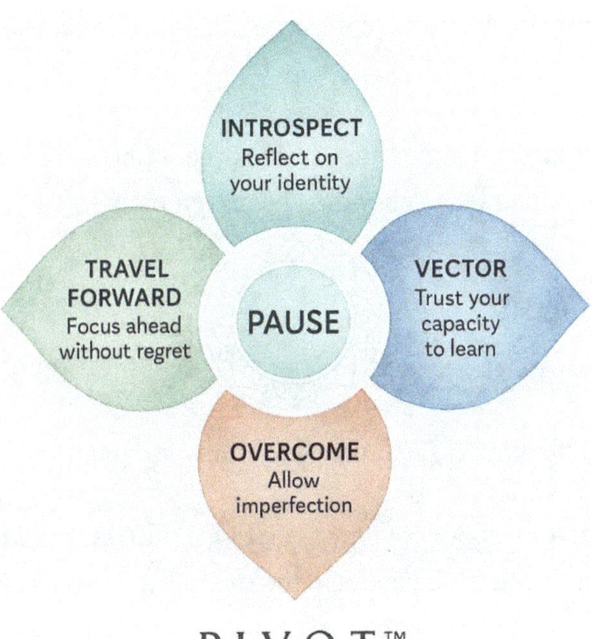

P — Pause

My first friction point was panic. My instinct was to rush, fix, and prove myself. But reacting from fear only deepened my exhaustion.

Pausing did not mean stopping my work or withdrawing from responsibility. It meant allowing myself to feel without immediately trying to solve. That small pause created space between fear and action.

The pause did not remove uncertainty. It prevented fear from becoming identity.

In that space, I learned that stillness could be a form of strength — a way to contain fear rather than be driven by it.

I — Introspect

Identity disruption sat at the heart of my struggle.

I had been a senior economist, a CEO, a professor. Suddenly, I was the least knowledgeable person in the room. I wrestled with questions like: Who am I if I am not excelling? How do I lead while still learning? What does competence look like now?

Introspection helped me separate who I am from what I do.

Over time, I realized I could be both a capable leader and a learner. My worth had not disappeared just because my environment had changed. This shift restored a sense of continuity — the feeling that I was still myself, even as my role evolved.

V — Vector

When it came time to actually perform the work, overwhelm hit hardest. Tasks felt impossible because I didn't yet understand the language or systems.

Vectoring meant directing my energy toward what I *could* do.

I broke tasks into smaller pieces and leaned on transferable strengths. I used my math skills to reconcile invoices even when the accounting system was unfamiliar to me. I relied on organization to create structure where none existed yet. I kept careful lists, centralized files, and built simple systems.

Each small success mattered. I quietly celebrated what I learned each day and week. Those small victories rebuilt my confidence because I trusted my ability to learn, even though I still didn't know much.

O — Overcome the Fear of Mistakes

The most draining source of friction was embarrassment.

I made mistakes — some small, some serious. At first, each one felt catastrophic. Over time, I learned to soften my self-talk. Nobody was replaying my errors the way I was. I could learn, correct, and move on.

Owning mistakes without dwelling on them freed enormous energy. These colleagues didn't know my past or my track record, which gave me unexpected freedom: the freedom to redefine myself without being trapped by who I had been.

Letting go of perfectionism accelerated learning and reduced self-criticism.

T — Travel Forward

Finally, I saw how much energy I was losing by clinging to what no longer existed — the career I had left, the identity I missed, the resentment I carried about being in a job I hadn't wanted.

The more I looked backward, the less present I was for what stood in front of me.

Traveling forward did not mean erasing the past. It meant releasing its grip.

When I focused on learning, adapting, and improving, the work stopped feeling like punishment. It became a challenge I could meet. By the end of my three-month trial period, the manager who once believed he would need to let me go asked me to stay. I had become indispensable — and I had done so without sacrificing my inner stability.

Why This Framework Matters

P.I.V.O.T.™ works because it restores the internal conditions that enable adaptability.

Rather than asking, *"How do we make environments safer?"* it asks, *"How do we help people feel steady enough inside themselves to meet what is being asked of them?"*

By calming reactivity, separating discomfort from identity, reconnecting people with their transferable strengths, softening self-judgment, and committing to the journey ahead, the framework empowers people in uncertain times.

From that grounded place, they can trust themselves again — learning, recovering, and course-correcting without needing certainty or permission. Over time, self-trust replaces self-protection.

This framework did not come from theory alone. It grew out of lived experience, shaped through reflection, and later strengthened through research and practice. At its heart is a simple human truth: **when we feel grounded again, forward movement becomes possible.**

In the chapters ahead, we will explore each part of P.I.V.O.T.™ more deeply. But first, it helps to understand why change unsettles us so quickly — and why our sense of meaning is often the first thing to wobble.

That is where we go next.

Chapter 6 — Sensemaking: How the Mind Interprets Change

Before we explore how to apply the P.I.V.O.T.™ Method, it helps to understand what is happening inside us when change shows up.

In the previous chapter, I shared how this framework was born from lived experience through trial and error during my season of desperation – my *tsunami*. I also explained what P.I.V.O.T.™ is and what it is not. At its core, it works internally to steady the mind when change disrupts our sense of direction, identity, or certainty. It works with the mind to make sense of what is changing and who people are becoming within the change.

To understand why this matters so much, we need to look at how the mind naturally responds to change.

Because change doesn't only alter our circumstances.
It unsettles how we make sense of what's happening.

And when understanding wobbles, fear often rushes in to fill the gap.

Underneath all of this is a simple human instinct: the mind wants things to make sense.

That instinct is called *sensemaking.*

This internal process of meaning-making is not something I encountered only through experience. Sensemaking theory was also the foundation of my doctoral research, when I studied how organizations make strategic decisions. I learned that people, often acting on behalf of organizations, make decisions based on their unique understanding of the world. I was later struck by how central these same concepts are in moments of change.

What Sensemaking Is

Sensemaking is how the mind tries to understand what's going on. It happens quietly and automatically, often without us noticing.

It shows up as questions we rarely say out loud, but rely on all the time:

What is happening?

What does this mean for me?

Who am I in this situation?

What should I do next?

Whenever something unexpected happens, the mind starts answering these questions right away. Most of the time, the answers come so quickly that we assume they are facts.

But they're not facts.

They're interpretations.

Sensemaking isn't about getting things "right."

It's about helping the mind feel oriented again.

In moments of uncertainty, the mind looks for something familiar to hold onto. It searches for patterns, old stories, or past experiences that make the situation feel understandable, even if those explanations no longer fully fit.

Why Change Feels So Unsettling

When change disrupts routines, roles, or expectations, the mind briefly loses its map. The story that used to navigate everyday life no longer works.

In that gap, the mind reaches for what feels familiar and safest — not what's most helpful.

It often falls back on familiar ideas like:

Uncertainty means danger.

Mistakes mean I'm not capable.

Waiting feels safer than moving.

Control equals security.

These ideas don't show up because they're true. They show up because they're familiar.

This is why change often feels emotional before it becomes logical. Our bodies respond to the story we're telling ourselves long before we've had time to examine whether it's true.

Sensemaking and Identity

Sensemaking isn't just about understanding events.

It's deeply tied to how we see ourselves.

We don't interpret change based only on what's happening.

We interpret it through who we believe we are.

A new role can shake our sense of competence. A new environment can challenge our sense of belonging. A learning curve can feel like a judgment on our worth.

When identity feels unsettled, everything feels heavier. Tasks feel harder. Feedback feels personal. Uncertainty feels threatening.

This is why two people can experience the same change and respond very differently. Their circumstances may look similar on the outside, but their inner stories are not.

How we see ourselves shapes how we interpret change.

How we interpret change shapes how we feel.

And how we feel shapes what we do next.

How Sensemaking Creates Momentum or Resistance

Once the mind settles on an interpretation, behavior follows quickly.

If change is interpreted as danger, we protect ourselves. We avoid, withdraw, resist, or try to control.

If change is interpreted as failure, we turn inward with doubt and self-criticism.

If change is interpreted as a possibility, curiosity becomes available. Learning feels safer. Engagement becomes possible.

In this way, sensemaking quietly determines whether we move forward or get stuck, often before we realize we have made a choice.

This is why so many change efforts stall early. The problem isn't the change itself. It's the **meaning** attached to it.

Where P.I.V.O.T.™ Enters the Process

P.I.V.O.T.™ was created to help restore meaning during the sense vacuum created by change.

Instead of asking people to push harder, stay positive, or act confident, the framework steadies the mind throughout the transition. It slows things down just enough to notice the story that's forming and then gently guides it toward empowering thoughts.

Change often unfolds like this:

1. Change disrupts meaning.
2. Disrupted meaning creates disorientation.
3. Disorientation gives rise to fear or resistance.
4. P.I.V.O.T.™ steps in before fear takes over.

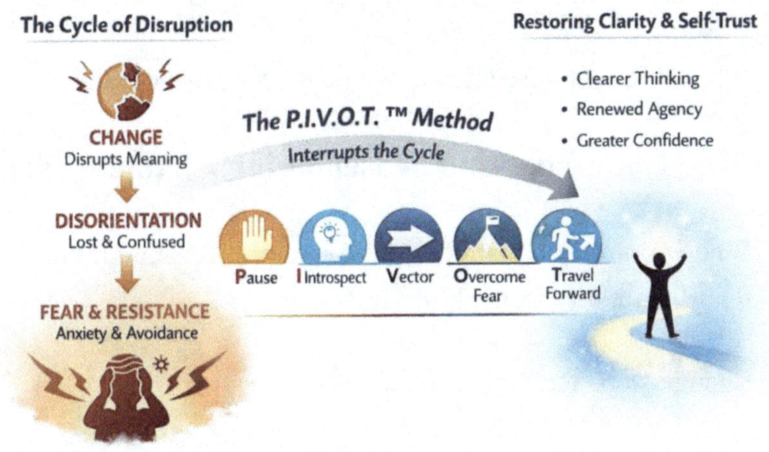

Each part of the framework supports a different moment in this process, a different *friction point*:

Pause creates space before reactions harden.

Introspect helps you notice how identity is shaping the story.

Vector reminds you of what you already know and can use.

Overcoming softens harsh self-judgment and reduces threat.

Travel Forward restores a sense of choice and momentum.

When meaning steadies, fear eases.

When orientation returns, movement becomes possible.

Why Understanding Sensemaking Changes Everything

When you realize that your mind interprets change rather than simply reporting reality, something shifts.

Change stops feeling personal.

It stops feeling like a verdict on your competence or worth.

It stops feeling like something you must conquer or control.

Instead, it becomes **something you can work with**.

Understanding sensemaking doesn't remove discomfort, but it helps you stop treating discomfort as danger.

It allows you to stay present with uncertainty instead of panicking, and to soften toward yourself rather than pushing or judging.

This is why P.I.V.O.T.™ works.

It doesn't impose meaning.

It supports the meaning-making that's already happening.

Now that you understand how the mind interprets change, we can take our first intentional step into the P.I.V.O.T.™ Method.

Every dance begins with a breath.

Every transition begins with a moment of stillness.

Every new interpretation begins with silence.

The first step is not movement — it's Pause.

Chapter 7 – Pause

Feel it before you fix it.

Every morning, as I opened my laptop to begin work at my new job—the job I needed but didn't want- I scanned the day's requirements. Often, I felt bewildered by how little I understood, not only of the tasks themselves but of the language being used. Panic rose quickly.

My response was almost automatic: act. Do something—*anything*. I told myself that movement was better than freezing, that action would bring clarity. In a fast-paced environment, visible output felt safer than sitting with uncertainty.

Over time, that instinct began to cost me. I made avoidable mistakes—not because I wasn't capable, but because I hadn't slowed down long enough to understand what was actually being asked. I hadn't gathered context. I hadn't thought clearly. Action had become my antidote to uncertainty, and it was no longer serving me.

Without fully realizing it at first, I began to pause whenever I felt unsure and resisted the urge to act.

That lesson was reinforced during my first performance review. My manager said, *"Khutso, I appreciate how fast and energetic you are.*

But you need to pause before acting. Take the time to read the emails fully. Make sure you understand before implementing solutions."

He was right. In fact, I had reached the same conclusion myself only days earlier.

So, I began pausing deliberately. I stopped before actioning. I noticed how much steadier I felt afterward. Pausing gave me time to reset, gather context, and respond with intention rather than urgency. That shift changed everything. It became my first lived practice of P.I.V.O.T.™—creating space before reaction.

As I practiced pausing, something unexpected happened. My confidence no longer came from knowing what to do. It came from trusting that I could figure things out. Pausing reconnected me with my own resourcefulness. It gave me access again to my intelligence, empathy, and creativity—qualities panic tends to shut down. I was often surprised by how clear my instincts became once I slowed down enough to listen.

We live in a culture that rewards speed: fast replies, quick decisions, instant results. But when change strikes, speed often becomes the enemy of progress. You can't dance if you're sprinting. You need rhythm, not rush. Pause allows rhythm to return.

Pausing is grounding. When we're shocked or overwhelmed, clear thinking is often the first thing to go. Even brief stillness helps the mind and body catch up with what's unfolding. Pause is how we reclaim choice from fear.

Pausing during moments of shock, however, can be deeply difficult. When the disruption lasts days or weeks, we often find ourselves fighting ourselves as anxiety and panic try to take over. Our brains can't help but jump to worst-case scenarios—and then stay there. Days can turn into months if we let them.

This is what I call the *negative thought circuit.*

Once trapped in it, the mind loops relentlessly. Composure erodes. Agency slips away. The body stays on high alert, even when no immediate action is required. This is where Pause becomes not just helpful—but essential.

Breaking the Negative Thought Circuit

Pausing can feel uncomfortable because it brings things to the surface we've been avoiding. Silence has a way of revealing fear, grief, or frustration we'd rather outrun. Busy minds resist the pause at all costs.

I learned this again very recently.

A few days ago, I was unexpectedly laid off. I arrived at work as usual, and by midday, I received the news that my role would end immediately.

As soon as I heard, I decided to follow the medicine I teach: **do nothing**.

I didn't even get out of my chair. I looked outside at the snow falling for a few minutes. I remember thinking, *I've never seen snow fall during work hours.*

Then my mind erupted.

What now? How will I feed the children? Will I be good enough for the next role? How long will it take to find another job? Do I tell people? Do I stay quiet?

The questions multiplied. Along with them came a heavy sense of doom.

I'm screwed. I'm going to get evicted. The debtors will hound me. We'll end up on the street.

Even as I paused repeatedly and felt calmer in my body, the thoughts were relentless for days. They slipped in whenever they could, tightening my chest and trying to hijack my mind.

In those moments, I remembered a simple tool I had learned from Dr. Joe Dispenza. When a negative thought loop takes over, saying the word **"change"** out loud can interrupt the pattern and create just enough space to refocus.

So, I added that to my pause.

It worked.

Not perfectly. Not permanently. But enough to break the momentum of the spiral.

I'll say this plainly: when I felt myself spiraling, saying—or even shouting—the word *change* helped interrupt the loop.

Any word can work. I've learned this from others who use the same technique. A good friend of mine uses the word *peace*.

You might discover a word of your own—one that feels grounding enough to reach for when your thoughts start to race.

And take as long as you need, without shame, for your pause.

It can be minutes.
It can be days.
It can even be months.

There is humility in pausing. It means admitting, *I don't know yet.* That phrase once frightened me. I used to hear failure in it. Now I hear possibility. When I allow myself not to know right away, I create space for learning, collaboration, and growth.

Pausing doesn't have to be dramatic. Sometimes it's a single breath. Sometimes it's sleeping on a decision. A pause before replying to an email. A moment of silence before responding to a comment. Sometimes it's allowing yourself weeks or months to process shock.

The world does not collapse when you pause. Often, it opens.

As my days of job uncertainty stretched on, I found it harder to stay grounded—even though I paused frequently and often used the word *change* to interrupt my negative thought circuit. I realized I needed additional reinforcements to steady myself.

My therapist offered another simple but effective practice: **counter the thoughts**.

If you can't stop negative thoughts from landing, counter them with evidence.

Mine tended to sound apocalyptic:

I'm never going to get another job I want.
Employers will think I'm overqualified.
I'm going to end up desolate again.

But the truth was, I had recent evidence that contradicted those fears. Within days of starting the application process, I had secured an interview. Someone had noticed my application almost immediately and thought I was worth shortlisting. The year before, I had been offered my ideal role.

Even though neither outcome had lasted, they still mattered. They were proof that my fears were not facts.

Countering my thoughts in this way didn't eliminate anxiety, but it softened its grip. It helped turn the spiral just enough to restore a sense of steadiness.

To dance with change is to learn the rhythm of stillness. Just as music relies on rests between notes, life relies on pauses between transitions. Those pauses don't interrupt the song. They give it shape.

Through the lens of P.I.V.O.T.™, **Pause** is a conscious choice to interrupt reactivity. It is choosing intention over impulse. With practice, it becomes a form of inner choreography, the first graceful step in your dance with change.

Reflection Prompts for Practicing the Pause

1. *Think of a recent situation that left you feeling overwhelmed. What might have changed if you had paused before responding?*
2. *What emotions tend to surface when you pause—fear, guilt, frustration, calm?*
3. *Where in your life do you confuse busyness with progress?*

4. *The next time you feel the urge to act quickly, take one slow breath and silently say, "I have time." Notice what happens.*

5. *How might you build small pauses into your day—moments to breathe, reflect, or reset?*

When you practice pausing, you begin to hear the rhythm of change more clearly—the rush quiets. The panic softens. **Pause is not the absence of movement. It is where alignment begins.**

As we continue our dance with change, the next step after pausing is to turn inward—to examine who we are within the movement.

That is where we go next: **Introspect.**

Chapter 8 – Introspect

Who you think you are affects what you do

That unexpected text from my last husband caught me completely off guard. It was the message in which he told me he no longer wanted to be in a relationship with me and, by extension, with my children. We had disagreed before, as any couple does, but nothing felt serious enough to explain this. I truly believed we had worked through our differences.

I couldn't believe it. From the outside, we looked happy. Friends admired our relationship. Some even called us "couple goals." I had no warning that he had been sitting with this decision long before he shared it with me.

When he said he was done, I didn't know how to respond. Should I plead for a chance to fix whatever I didn't understand? Or should I accept it with dignity and walk away? I chose confirmation first. We met in person, and he confirmed that he was finished.

The first thought that crossed my mind was simple and devastating: *Who am I now?*

I had been his wife for four years, his partner for much longer. That identity had quietly wrapped itself around how I saw myself and how I moved through the world. I didn't know how I would explain this ending to others. Beneath the shock, what I felt most was *shame.*

Shame for failing at yet another meaningful relationship. Shame at the thought of returning, once again, to the label of "single mother." I had taken his last name as a public symbol of our shared life. Now I had to let his last name go — a public loss he didn't have to carry, since he had never taken mine.

When my survival instincts took over, I reached for what had always helped me before: movement and planning. I reminded myself who I had been before this relationship: a global, independent woman with a full life and big dreams. I decided to reconnect with that version of myself. I was no longer someone's wife. I was, once again, simply **me**.

Change has a way of shaking our sense of self. When something ends or shifts, the question "Who am I now?" often follows close behind.

We attach parts of our identity to roles, titles, and relationships without realizing it. So, when those fall away, it can feel as though the ground beneath us has disappeared.

Introspection is how we find our footing again.

It's the quiet practice of looking inward and asking honest questions: *What part of me was tied to this role? What am I afraid of losing? Who am I without it?*

Those questions aren't comfortable. But they open the door to freedom.

I faced a similar identity reckoning when I started my new job soon after I immigrated to the United States — the job I needed but didn't want and barely understood.

Most days, I felt out of place. What unsettled me most wasn't the learning curve itself, but the gap between who I believed myself to be and what I was doing at work. I have two master's degrees, a doctorate, years as a CEO, and experience teaching at the university level. Yet here I was, doing entry-level work and struggling to keep up.

The tension became sharper after I completed my doctorate. I wanted to be recognized for it. I wanted to add it to my email signature, but that didn't fit the role I was in, so I hid it instead.

What finally eased the strain was a simple realization: no one here knew my past, and that was okay.

I told myself, *"This role pays the bills. It does not define my worth. What I'm doing today is not who I am."*

That shift allowed me to breathe again. I stopped fighting myself. I gave my full attention to the work before me and appreciated the stability it provided. Introspection helped me loosen my grip on an identity that no longer fit.

This is the power of introspection.

It asks us to separate ourselves from what we do. It helps us notice where pride, fear, or the need for validation might be shaping our resistance to change.

When we skip this step, we often fight battles that aren't really about growth but about *image*.

Every major transition invites this choice: cling to an old version of yourself or make room for a new one.

The tighter we hold on to an identity that no longer fits, the heavier change feels. When we loosen that hold, energy returns. Movement becomes possible again.

It sounds like gentle truth-telling:
What am I afraid of losing?
What story am I telling myself about who I should be?
Is that story still serving me?

When we ask these questions honestly, change stops feeling like something that happens to us. It becomes something we participate in.

Reflection Prompts for Practicing Introspection

1. Think of a change you are currently navigating. Who do you believe

yourself to be within that change?
2. What part of your identity feels threatened by this transition?
3. What story about yourself might you need to update or release to move forward with peace?
4. Recall a moment when you surprised yourself by adapting better than you expected. What did that reveal about your true resilience?
5. How might embracing a new or evolving identity open possibilities you couldn't see before?

Introspection is also an act of compassion. It's not about judging yourself. It's about seeing yourself clearly, without harshness. When we learn to introspect, we turn confrontation into collaboration. We no longer fear who we are becoming. We take part in that becoming.

Introspection is how we meet ourselves again after life has shifted the mirror.

Once we have steadied our sense of who we are, we're ready for the next step — to *vector*. To use what we already know to learn what's new.

The dance continues.

Chapter 9 – Vector

You already have what you need.

Every morning at this job I needed but didn't want to feel like stepping into a storm without shelter. I didn't just lack answers; I lacked language. Words I thought I understood carried completely different meanings in this new world. I often felt lost before the day had even begun.

I was stunned by how disoriented I felt. How could I — someone with more than twenty-five years of professional experience — struggle with tasks that seemed basic to everyone else? How could I — a former university professor, fluent in language — not even understand what was being said around me? The gap between who I had been and how I was showing up was humbling.

But I needed the job. And to keep it, I needed to find a way to be useful.

That necessity forced a shift. Instead of focusing on everything I didn't know, I asked a simpler question: *What can I contribute right now?*

I began with what I already knew how to do. I noticed the newly formed team lacked basic organization. So, I stepped in. I read every email carefully. I saved documents in one shared place. I flagged missing information and clarified next steps. I relied on my natural ability to organize and communicate clearly.

When it came time to learn the complex software at the center of the role, I didn't start from scratch even though it felt like I had. The systems were very different from anything I had used before, but I approached learning like building with Lego: I searched for even the smallest pieces that looked familiar and used them to make sense of what I didn't yet understand. I learned slowly, piece by piece, comparing the new with the known until patterns began to emerge.

I also leaned into who I am. I brought warmth and humility into the room. I asked questions. I owned my mistakes. I used lightness to soften moments of frustration. That combination — competence where I had it, and grace where I didn't — helped ease tension with colleagues who were struggling to teach someone new.

Over time, something important clicked. I realized I wasn't failing at learning, and I didn't have to be overwhelmed by it. I was learning exactly the way learning actually happens — step by step, with reference points, through trial and error.

I already had what it took to learn.

That realization is the heart of *Vector*.

A vector is the moment you remember that learning is possible because you are not starting from nothing. You already have experience, personality, skills, instincts, and ways of thinking you can draw from.

When change hits, the mind often panics. Unfamiliar territory feels like danger. Vector interrupts that fear by reminding the mind: *We've navigated the unknown before. We can do it again.*

That reassurance shifts you out of survival mode and back into learning capability. From that steadier place, creativity returns. So does confidence.

In work, Vector sounds like, "I don't know this yet, but I can figure it out."
In relationships, it's the moment you stop asking, "Why is this happening to me?" and start asking, "What can I learn here?"
In life transitions, it's about trusting that even without answers, you can find them.

Reflection Prompts for Practicing Vector

1. Think of a situation that feels intimidating right now. What part of it is already familiar to you, even in a small way?
2. What skills or experiences from your past could help you learn what's new?
3. When was the last time you learned something under pressure? What helped you through it?

4. What could you remind yourself of today to reinforce that you are capable of learning?
5. How does it feel to replace "I can't do this" with "I can learn this"?

Vector is empowering because it restores agency. It reminds you that you are not powerless or behind. You are equipped. That knowledge, in itself, is freedom.

There is one important truth to name here: learning requires trying. And trying inevitably involves mistakes.

Vector gives you the courage to begin. But as you stretch into the unfamiliar, another challenge quickly appears — the fear of getting it wrong.

That is where we turn next.

Chapter 10 – Overcome the Fear of Making Mistakes

Overcome the Suck!

Just when I thought I was finally getting the hang of my job, everything changed again.

It had been a little over a year since I started. The early chaos had settled. I understood the language. I knew my team. We worked well together. I was sleeping again. I could finally breathe.

Then my manager told me our unit would be dissolved.

At first, I felt relief because he assured me I wasn't losing my job. We would be absorbed into other teams. Beneath that relief, though, anxiety crept in. I had just earned my doctorate and hoped to put it to use. Once again, I chose security over an ideal role.

When I arrived in the new position, I assumed some things would carry over from the old one. *I was wrong.* The environment was different. The expectations were different. The rules were different.

The only difference this time was internal.

I had learned how to steady myself. I knew how to pause. I knew how to separate my identity from the role. I trusted my ability to learn. Even so, I hit a familiar wall.

Mistakes.

I made them again — both small and serious. I misunderstood hierarchies. I missed protocols. Some errors could have cost the company money. I was mortified.

Every day brought a new reason to cringe. I replayed my missteps at night and woke up dreading the next workday. I worked weekends to catch up and correct errors, all while raising three children alone in a foreign country.

Inside, I was relentless with myself. I was convinced everyone saw me as incompetent. That belief built quietly until one weekend, my body gave in.

One Sunday morning, I woke up shaking at the thought of going back to work. I broke down crying. Before my children woke up, I called my doctor's office. They were closed. The nurse referred me to a 24-hour mental health facility.

I spent the day there, letting go of fear, pressure, and the need to prove myself.

I was signed off work for two weeks.

When I returned, something had shifted.

I decided I would no longer take the job so personally. It was work, not a verdict on my worth. No one was cataloging my mistakes the way I was. I wasn't saving lives. I was learning, and it was inevitable that I would suck at something new.

That simple reframing brought immediate relief.

I stopped assuming everyone was watching and judging me. I stopped fearing future mistakes. I even began naming my imperfections out loud, often with humor. I'd joke, "Let me double-check — you know I'm the one who always makes mistakes." People laughed. The tension eased.

And with that, the fear lost its grip.

That's when I understood something important: *overcoming* isn't about perfection. It's about perspective.

The moment you stop trying to prove your competence, you recover your energy to grow. When you laugh at your own missteps, shame loosens its hold. You become lighter. Freer. More human.

Humor creates distance between you and the mistake. It allows you to see yourself with kindness instead of cruelty. And from that place, learning becomes easier.

Once fear quiets, clarity returns.

This is the paradox of overcoming. When the inner critic steps aside, the learner can finally step forward.

Overcome is permission to be both capable and imperfect at once. It's letting go of the belief that mistakes define you and recognizing that they are simply part of the process of becoming.

Reflection Prompts for Practicing Overcoming

1. Think of a recent mistake that still lingers in your mind. What might change if you met it with a bit more humor?
2. What story are you telling yourself about what others think of your mistakes?
3. How often do you judge yourself more harshly than anyone else ever has?
4. What might feel different if mistakes became information instead of evidence against you?
5. What gentle phrase could you offer yourself the next time you get something wrong?

When you overcome the fear of making mistakes, you stop tiptoeing around change. You move more freely. You participate more fully.

But overcoming fear is not the final step. Once fear loosens its grip, a new question emerges: *Now what?*

That's where we go next.

Travel Forward is about what happens when you stop rehearsing the past and start building what comes next. It's about moving ahead, not perfectly, but intentionally.

The dance continues.

Chapter 11 – Travel Forward

Don't Look Back!

Those first few days at my new job after I moved to the United States were grueling. Mind you, I knew nothing about the job – I didn't even want it really – but I needed it. It was soon after starting this job that I found myself facing an excruciating legal battle that lasted over 2 years. In those 2 years, leaving my job was not an option.

During those early days, I noticed most of the turmoil I was feeling was due to wishing things were different. I wish I had gotten a more suitable, better-paying job. Wishing I hadn't been so quick to accept this one. Wishing I had never quit the stable (but boring) job I had had as an economist in South Africa years before I left the country. Wishing life wasn't so hard. Regretting everything I did and said that seemed like a bad move or a mistake. Wishing I were not where I was – professionally and otherwise.

I beat myself up about it, especially as I was weighing whether I would try to find another job or stay. I distinctly remember the day I decided to stay. The day I decided to make myself indispensable at this job, so that I wouldn't give them a reason to kick me out until I was ready to go. The minute I made that decision, I felt instant relief. I no longer fought myself. I no longer tormented myself with all the wishes. I only focused on my new goal: to stay at all costs. I invested all my energy in finding ways to help myself reach that goal, rather than diverting it by vacillating between directions and contradictory goals.

In deciding to focus ahead rather than behind, I realized I felt more at peace. I was able to embrace my new life more easily. I was able to learn faster without resistance. My lesson to myself was: Travel forward and don't look back!

Travel Forward is the culmination of the P.I.V.O.T.™ journey. It is the moment when resilience becomes rhythm. It's the shift from reaction to creation, from surviving change to shaping it. To travel forward is to decide a direction for your new story and to commit to it.

Every journey of transformation reaches a point where looking back costs more energy than moving ahead. The past no longer needs to be fought, fixed, or justified. It simply needs to be integrated.

When we Travel Forward, we stop negotiating with what could have been and begin collaborating with what is. This shift doesn't deny loss or difficulty. It simply refuses to keep arguing with reality.

In psychological research, this orientation is associated with greater adaptability and resilience. People who learn to loosen their grip on alternate outcomes and redirect their energy toward what's available now tend to recover from upheaval faster and report higher levels of well-being. That is because even though uncertainty does not disappear, it's no longer treated as an obstacle.

In this way, Travel Forward is not about optimism. It's about commitment.

It's the choice to stop splitting attention between what no longer exists and what now requires engagement. Travel Forward releases the mental tug-of-war with the past and redirects energy toward the work, relationships, and possibilities that are actually in front of us. Nothing has to feel resolved for movement to begin — focus comes first, and clarity follows through action.

When you choose to travel forward, you also release regret and reclaim momentum. You let the story breathe and evolve. You permit yourself to live the next chapter without rewriting the last.

Reflection Prompts for Traveling Forward

1. *What situations in your life still pull your thoughts backward?*
2. *How would it feel to stop fighting those memories and simply let them rest where they are?*

3. *What might "traveling forward" look like in this season of your life—one small step at a time?*

4. *What part of your story are you ready to thank and release?*

5. *How might you remind yourself that peace doesn't require perfection—just direction?*

Travel Forward is not about pretending the past didn't happen. It's about remembering that it no longer holds you hostage. It's about learning to move with the rhythm of change – forward, not against it. Every pivot forward creates new space for joy, discovery, and alignment.

After all, dancing with change isn't just about finding balance. It's about remembering that forward is a direction, not a destination.

PART II: THE APPLICATIONS

PERSONAL TRANSFORMATIONS

The Dance Begins With You

Every pivot leads somewhere — not back to who we were, but toward who we are becoming.

When I look back now, I can see that every struggle, every unexpected turn, every *"I can't do this* moment" was quietly shaping what would later become the P.I.V.O.T.™ Method. It wasn't designed in a boardroom or sketched out on a whiteboard. It was forged in the messy, unplanned choreography of real life in moments when nothing felt stable, certain, or clear.

That's why this work begins here.

Before P.I.V.O.T.™ shows up in our leadership, our work, or our institutions, it shows up in who we are when life disrupts us personally: when identity shifts, when relationships change, when the inner rules we've been living by no longer hold.

Chapters 12 and 13 explore P.I.V.O.T.™ at this most intimate level.

Not as a self-improvement tool, but as a way of re-orienting the mind when familiar patterns stop working, when goals collide with identity, and endings ask us to become someone new.

These chapters focus on *personal* recalibration:

- updating inner rules without erasing yourself
- releasing identities that once protected you but now exhaust you
- learning to trust your capacity to adapt, again and again.

This is where the dance begins — not on a stage, but inside you.

Because change will keep coming.

And so will you.

The mind that can pause, introspect, vector, overcome, and travel forward is not fragile. It is adaptable. It is resilient. It knows how to move without fighting itself.

As you turn the page, I invite you to make P.I.V.O.T.™ your own. Test it. Notice how it shows up in your thoughts, your reactions, your inner dialogue. Let it become less of a framework you remember and more of a rhythm you return to.

What follows are invitations to apply P.I.V.O.T.™ across different areas of life, beginning with personal transformation, and then extending outward into relationships, leadership, education, and organizational change.

This is not the end of the dance.

It's the moment you step onto the floor.

Chapter 12: P.I.V.O.T.™ Into a New You

How many times do we resolve to make changes we genuinely want and then find ourselves repeating the same patterns anyway?

Get healthier.
Get a new job.
Work harder. Or finally rest.
Save more money. Wake up earlier. Let go more.

These goals are sincere, and when they don't stick, it's rarely because the change is too big or the intention isn't real. More often, it's because the change quietly asks us to stop being who we believe we are.

Many of us live from identities we formed early: *I'm the strong one. I'm easygoing. I'm the peacemaker. I'm not a morning person.* These identities are not flaws. They are adaptations — ways we learned to survive, succeed, or belong. Like all adaptations, they sometimes need to change.

When a goal contradicts one of these identities, the mind resists — not because the change is difficult, but because it feels unfamiliar or unsafe. A goal like waking up earlier, saving more money, or asking for help can quietly fail, not because it's difficult. Still, because it contradicts an unspoken identity — *"I'm not a morning person," "I'm generous", "I'm the one who handles things alone."*

Those identities come with inner rules. Unspoken assumptions about what is possible, what is safe, and what kind of person we are allowed to be. They shape how we see ourselves and the world around us, guiding our choices long before we consciously decide anything at all, until life pushes back hard enough for us to notice them.

Psychologists sometimes call these inner rules *paradigms* — the lenses we don't realize we're living inside.

When the way you see the world changes, the way you move through it changes too. Over time, that doesn't just reshape your habits — it reshapes who you are.

I was forced into that kind of inner reckoning in ways I hadn't anticipated.

For years, I took pride in being a strong, independent woman. I regarded myself as fiercely independent — hyper-independent, really. I made decisions from that place. I carried everything alone. I avoided asking for help because I believed that seeking support diminished my worth, competence, and strength.

That way of living served me, until it didn't.

I share that story in detail in my earlier book, *No More Free Passes*. Here, I want to offer a different moment — one that shows how an old way of operating can quietly become unsustainable, and how a shift in inner orientation can change everything.

My Identity P.I.V.O.T.™

It started with another email — one more task added to a plate that was already balancing on the thinnest edge of my sanity. My heart was pounding before I even opened it. My palms were sweating. My team was in transition, everything shifting by the minute, and I was trying to keep pace as if my life depended on it.

"This is corporate," I whispered to myself, attempting to steady the rising panic. "You get paid reasonably well, so you work like a machine. You hold it together. You do everything — and you do it flawlessly — because you cannot afford to look incompetent." That was the script I had rehearsed for years.

I had a subordinate assigned to support me, but even the thought of involving her made the knot in my stomach tighten. Delegating felt like more work, not less. I would need to train her, monitor her, quality-check her output — and likely redo half of it — because I was not willing to risk my reputation on work that wasn't perfect.

Who has time to do a task twice?

So instead, I did it all myself.

I worked late nights without compensation. I took on every assignment quietly, efficiently, invisibly — the way hyper-independent people do. And because I delivered good work under impossible circumstances, more kept coming my way. I was capable. I wasn't complaining. So the load doubled. Then tripled. Then became the norm.

Until one Sunday morning, when my body told the truth my mouth had refused to say.

I found myself facing the very outcome I believed hyper-independence would protect me from — not because I lacked competence, but because I was afraid to ask for help. Afraid to delegate. Afraid to let anyone see that the work, in fact, was too much.

Hyper-independence had always felt like strength.
But in the end, it was the most fragile place I had ever lived.

Hyper-independence disguises itself as competence, responsibility, and excellence — especially in seasons when the stakes feel high. But beneath that polished strength is a quieter truth: we fear that if we loosen our grip, even briefly, everything will fall apart. We don't trust others. We don't trust the process. And at the deepest level, we don't trust ourselves to survive disappointment again.

At some point, many of us arrive at a similar crossroads — not only with hyper-independence, but with other identities we've been living from. The ways we've learned to work, cope, lead, save, strive, or endure may no longer fit who we are becoming. Something in us knows it's time to relate differently.

What follows is not a formula for eliminating hyper-independence, nor a claim that it needs to be "fixed." It is an illustration of how P.I.V.O.T.™ can be used to loosen an old way of operating and create space for a new one.

In the sections ahead, P.I.V.O.T.™ is applied to hyper-independence as one example — a way of showing how we can meet familiar inner patterns with more awareness, choice, and self-trust, and then redirect our energy toward the direction we want to grow.

P.I.V.O.T.™ Application:

Using hyper-independence as one illustration of a broader inner shift

The same P.I.V.O.T.™ process described in earlier chapters can be used whenever an old inner rule tightens its grip whether that rule says *do it all yourself, avoid discomfort, don't speak up,* or *wait until you feel ready.* By pausing, reflecting on identity, redirecting existing strengths, softening the fear of imperfection, and committing your energy forward, you loosen what no longer serves you and make room for a new way of being.

Pause — Stop tightening. Let your body admit: "This is too much."

Hyper-independence teaches you to override the signals that say you're overwhelmed. Pausing interrupts that autopilot. It allows your nervous system to step out of emergency mode and into a state of honesty.

Why This Helps:

Because hyper-independence is a reaction; not a personality. The moment you pause, you interrupt the survival reflex that says, "I must do this alone or something bad will happen."

Examples:

- Instead of pushing through the email that spikes your anxiety, you place your hands on the desk, breathe, and name the feeling honestly: "I'm stretched thin."
- Before accepting the extra project automatically, you pause long enough to feel your own limits before committing.

Introspect — Ask: Who Am I Becoming Beyond the Version of Me That Carried Everything Alone?

Hyper-independence is not just a habit. It becomes an identity. A persona. A self-definition.

During introspection, you explore who you had to be to survive old seasons and who you are being called to become now.

Questions to guide your introspection:

- *Who was the version of me that believed asking for help was dangerous?*

- *What environments taught me that needing support made me weak or burdensome?*

- *What did hyper-independence protect me from?*

- *Is this identity still worthy of carrying into my next chapter?*

- *Who do I need to become now — a person who feels safe enough to let life support them?*

Why This Helps:

Because once you see why that earlier version of you needed hyper-independence, you can bless them for their service and gently release them.

Examples:

- You realize that the "I'll do it all myself" persona was built during seasons where you lacked consistent support.

- You notice that your identity as "the strong one" was formed in environments where vulnerability wasn't safe — and now you choose differently.

Vector — Use What You Already Know to Learn a New Way

Hyper-independent people are not weak; they are highly capable. Vectoring reminds you that you already have what you need to learn how to receive, delegate, and trust selectively.

Why This Helps:

Because you don't need to become someone else; you only need to redirect the discipline, intelligence, and reliability you already have.

Examples:

- You use your organizational skills not just to manage your workload, but to map out what can be delegated.

- You repurpose your attention to detail toward training someone once, so you don't have to redo everything forever.

Overcome — Release the Fear of Being Seen in Your Humanity

Hyper-independence thrives on the belief that being seen struggling makes you unworthy. Overcoming is the soft, compassionate work of dismantling that lie.

Why This Helps:

Because hyper-independent people don't fear work; they fear judgment. And judgment loses its power when you stop performing perfection.

Examples:

- You allow yourself to say: "I'm overloaded and need help."
- You delegate a task and resist the urge to redo it unless necessary.

Travel Forward — Take One Step That Lets Life Support You

Traveling forward means choosing a new direction to commit to — one where your strength flows instead of hardens.

Why This Helps:

Because change happens in movement, not in standing still.

Examples:

- You ask a colleague to take the first draft.
- You share the load at home instead of silently doing everything.

Reflection Prompts

1. *What story do I tell myself about asking for help?*
2. *What am I afraid people will think of me if they see I'm overwhelmed?*
3. *Which part of me still believes that doing everything alone makes me valuable?*
4. *Where in my life am I ready to stop over-functioning?*
5. *What small act of receiving can I practice this week?*

Closing Thoughts

The ways you learned to move through the world, whether they once protected you or simply helped you function, served a purpose in their time. Some identities were forged in survival. Others emerged through habit, preference, or repetition. None of them were mistakes.

But no identity is meant to remain fixed forever.

When you P.I.V.O.T.™, you are not erasing who you are or judging who you've been. You are updating the inner rules that shape how you see yourself and the world — releasing what no longer fits and keeping what still serves you.

This is how change begins to hold.
Not by forcing new behaviors onto an old self-image, but by allowing your sense of who you are to evolve without fighting yourself in the process and paying the cost of exhaustion or burnout over time.

You were never designed to live inside rigid definitions.
You were designed to adapt, recalibrate, and dance with life as it changes.

Chapter 13: P.I.V.O.T.™ Out of Relationships

From Holding On to Letting Go With Dignity

If you are a certain age, chances are you have already lived through one of these: the breakup.

Whether it ended abruptly or slowly, whether you chose it or it chose you, the ending of a relationship is rarely simple. Even when you know something is no longer working, the separation still shocks the nervous system. It rearranges routines, expectations, and quiet assumptions about the future. It touches pride, hope, and a sense of safety all at once.

With time, sometimes after weeks, months, or even years of wrestling, you wake up one morning and realize you aren't waiting for their message anymore. The ache softens into clarity. Not because the relationship didn't matter, but because the mind has stopped bargaining with what is.

This chapter is about that earlier phase when the wound is fresh, and the mind feels desperate to undo reality.

Can we dance with this painful change, too?

Is there a way to take off the edge when it feels like life has pulled the rug from underneath us?

When Love Ends, Identity Often Panics

Relationship endings don't only break hearts. They disrupt identity.

We don't just love; we attach meaning to love. Inner stories quietly form:

• If I'm chosen, I'm safe.
• If they stay, I'm worthy.
• If this ends, I failed.
• If I let go, I'll be alone forever.
• If I don't fix it, I'm not enough.

These are not irrational thoughts. They are inner rules. They are conclusions the mind once formed to feel protected.

When a relationship ends, those inner rules feel threatened. The mind reaches, replays, searches for explanations, and chases certainty. That impulse is human, but it can trap us in a loop, seeking relief from what is no longer available.

This is where P.I.V.O.T.™ helps — not by making heartbreak painless, but by stabilizing the inner world long enough to heal with dignity.

An Identity in Motion

What shocked me most was not the breakup itself, but how quickly my mind turned the ending into a verdict about my worth.

I remember staring at my phone late at night, refreshing messages that never came, replaying conversations, filling silence with imagined explanations.

I wasn't only grieving a person. I was grieving a version of myself I had been inside that relationship — the one who felt anchored and certain.

As that identity slipped, my mind reached for anything: a final conversation, a softer ending, a clearer reason. Heartbreak doesn't just hurt. It activates old inner rules that once promised safety.

Many of us reach similar crossroads not only in romantic relationships, but in friendships, family bonds, and partnerships that change shape. The relationship may be ending, loosening, or revealing that it can no longer hold them or us as we or they once were.

What follows is not a formula for getting over someone quickly. It is an illustration of how P.I.V.O.T.™ supports the mind when it spirals so you can move through endings with more self-trust and less self-judgment.

P.I.V.O.T.™ Application:

Using relationship endings as one illustration of a broader inner shift

Pause — Don't Chase the Void. Let the Silence Exist.

When a relationship ends, the instinct is to fill the emptiness. We want to explain, fix, plead, or prove. Pausing interrupts that reflex.

Say to yourself:

"I don't need to rush for relief. I can let this moment breathe."

Why This Helps:

Heartbreak creates urgency but urgency is not truth. Pausing signals safety and reminds the mind that pain can be felt without panic.

Examples:

- Instead of sending the message you'll regret later, you put the phone down and breathe.

- When the urge for immediate closure arises, you remind yourself, "I can live one day without answers."

Introspect — Ask: What Part of Me Thinks This Ending Defines Me?

Ask:

"Who was I trying to be in this relationship, and what was I trying to earn?"

Why This Helps:

Naming the identity beneath the attachment separates the ending from your value.

Examples:

• You notice how much energy went into being easy or agreeable.
• You realize part of you believed love had to be earned, and now you question that rule.

Vector — Remember Who You Were Before the Relationship and What You Learned

Say:

"I have lived without this person before, and I have also grown while being with them. What I learned in this relationship belongs to me now. I can carry it forward."

Why This Helps:

Vectoring reconnects you with your latent capabilities — including those that were strengthened or revealed through the relationship itself.

The relationship may have shaped you, but it did not create you. What you became there is now part of who you are everywhere.

Examples:

- You recognize that the confidence, communication, or self-respect you developed in the relationship didn't disappear when it ended, and you begin using it in your life now.
- You remember earlier seasons of independence *and* notice new capacities that emerged through intimacy, allowing both to steady you as you move forward.

Overcome — Release the Need to Judge Your Love

Say:
"Loving deeply was never the mistake."

Why This Helps:

Breakups often trigger harsh self-judgment and endless replaying of what went wrong. Compassion interrupts that inner trial and allows the heart to grieve without turning love into something shameful.

Examples:

• When embarrassment surfaces, you remind yourself, *"Caring was never a flaw."*
• When an old argument replays, you interrupt it with, *"I don't need to prosecute the past to heal."*

Travel Forward — Commit to Building a Life That Doesn't Require Their Return

Say:

"This chapter shaped me, but it does not decide my future."

Why This Helps:

Closure is often not a conversation. It is a decision to invest attention in the future.

Examples:

- You create a new routine where their presence once filled the space.
- When memories arise, you breathe and say, "That chapter is complete."

Reflection Prompts

- *What inner rule is this ending challenging?*

- *What role did I overplay — and what did it cost me?*
- *What lesson am I ready to keep without the pain?*
- *Where am I still trying to earn closure?*
- *What small step forward can I take this week?*

Closing Thought

Not every relationship is meant to last but every relationship reveals something.

Some reveal what you need.
Some reveal what you've outgrown.
Some reveal where you abandoned yourself and where you are ready to return.

When an ending arrives, your work is not to prove your worth or negotiate your way back into uncertainty.

Your work is to return to yourself.

Pause.
Introspect.
Vector.
Overcome.
Travel Forward.

That is how heartbreak becomes wisdom and endings become doorways, not punishments.

PROFESSIONAL APPLICATIONS

When the Inner Shift Meets the World

Something important has shifted.

You've moved through change at its most personal level — where identity loosens, inner rules surface, and familiar patterns begin to release. In Chapters 12 and 13, P.I.V.O.T.™ was applied to moments that don't announce themselves as "growth": the quiet unraveling of who we've been, and the subtle courage it takes to become someone new.

What happens next is not a departure from that work — it's an extension of it.

The chapters that follow turn outward, beginning with one of the most common arenas where personal and professional identities collide: **our careers**. Because the same inner recalibration required to release an old self or relationship is often what makes career pivots feel so destabilizing and so necessary.

As people began applying P.I.V.O.T.™ in their own lives, this is what they noticed:

"It felt like the message arrived at exactly the moment I needed it. P.I.V.O.T.™ helped me make sense of change in a way that felt manageable instead of overwhelming."
— Dentist

"P.I.V.O.T.™ made me realize that moving forward doesn't require going back to who you used to be. You don't live there anymore — and that realization was freeing."
— Educator

"I now catch myself and P.I.V.O.T.™ when things feel uncertain. It's become something I return to in real moments, not just in theory."
— University Student

What these reflections have in common is not the setting — education, healthcare, or personal life — but the same inner mechanism.

When the mind stabilizes, people stop resisting change.
They stop fighting themselves.
They stop exhausting their energy trying to regain what's already gone.

And that inner shift changes how change unfolds everywhere else.

Part III explores what happens when this inner work meets the world in careers, leadership roles, classrooms, and organizations navigating disruption. The framework does not change. Only the arena does.

P.I.V.O.T.™ is not a personal tool *or* a professional one.
It is a human one.

As you turn the page, you'll see how the same mental recalibration that supports personal transitions can be applied to collective ones — helping individuals, teams, and leaders navigate change with less fear, more clarity, and greater agency.

The dance does not stop here.
It widens.

Chapter 14: P.I.V.O.T.™ Through Career Transitions

From Stability to Self-Trust

It didn't happen all at once.

There was no dramatic resignation letter or grand announcement. Just a growing awareness that the life I was living on paper no longer reflected the one I was inhabiting internally. The role that once felt like an achievement now felt like a costume — impressive, familiar, and increasingly uncomfortable.

I kept wearing it because it worked. Because it paid the bills. Because it made sense to others.

One morning, staring at yet another list of tasks, I whispered, "I think I've outgrown this." The sentence terrified and freed me at the same time. For the first time, I realized I wasn't walking away from something broken. I was confronting a mismatch between who I had become and the inner rules I was still living by.

This time, I had a choice. I chose to leave.

But many career transitions don't arrive that gently. Layoffs, restructures, and relocations often land without warning. When your livelihood is at stake, the mind reacts quickly. Even when we dislike our work, the stability it provides can feel safer than the uncertainty that follows.

That's why so many people stay in roles that drain them. Not because they lack courage, but because the mind equates stability with survival.

I did that. I stayed at the job I didn't want for four years before the job unceremoniously laid me off. Completely unannounced.

So, the question becomes:
How do we steady ourselves when work changes — or ends — and our sense of security is shaken?

When Careers Disrupt Identity

Careers don't just shape schedules. They shape identity.

Over time, roles harden into self-definitions. Titles become shorthand for worth. Paychecks become proof of competence. Stability becomes safety even when the cost is quite high, such as exhaustion.

When a career shift occurs, chosen or forced, disruption isn't only practical. It's psychological. The mind scrambles to regain footing. It wants certainty. It wants replacement. It wants reassurance that nothing essential has been lost.

That reaction is human.

When the shock of losing work unsettles our sense of safety, the mind looks for immediate relief. If that inner disruption isn't steadied first, even small decisions can feel overwhelming.

This is where P.I.V.O.T.™ becomes essential — not as a job-search strategy, but as a mental recalibration that allows you to move through career change without fighting yourself in the process.

P.I.V.O.T.™ Application

Using career transitions as one illustration of a broader inner shift

Pause — Don't Fill the Gap with Panic

When work becomes unstable, the instinct is often to act immediately. Update your résumé. Search for certainty. Explain the ending. Prove your value.
Pausing interrupts that reflex.

Why Pausing Helps

Urgency often feels productive, but it usually comes from fear. Pausing creates a buffer between what happens *to* us and what we do *next*. It allows the nervous system to settle, so decisions are not made out of panic, scarcity, or self-doubt. Pause is not avoidance. It is containment.

Examples

- After a role ends unexpectedly, you resist the urge to explain, fix, or plan. You sit. You breathe. You let the moment land before assigning meaning to it.

- In the space between jobs, you notice the impulse to immediately update your résumé or reach out to contacts — and you choose to wait. Not forever. Just long enough for your body to calm and your thoughts to slow.

- When fear starts racing ahead to worst-case scenarios, you stop engaging the questions altogether. You don't answer them. You don't argue with them. You simply pause.

Introspect — Separate Who You Are from What You Do

Career transitions expose how tightly identity can become fused with role.

Ask yourself:

"What part of my worth have I tied to this job?"
"What part of me do I genuinely want to express in my next role?"

Remember: **a job is a role you perform — not the definition of who you are.**

Why This Helps:

When identity is anchored solely in productivity or title, change can feel deeply threatening. Introspection restores a fuller sense of self—one that can adapt and move forward without collapsing.

Examples:

• You realize you weren't just a manager; you were someone who built trust, solved problems, and supported growth.
• You remind yourself: The role expressed me. It did not define me.

Vector — Remember What You Already Know How to Do

Career endings often feel like a loss. Vector reframes them as evidence that you have already built skills, judgment, and experience you can carry forward.

Say to yourself:

"Every skill I've learned still belongs to me, and I can use it to learn my new role."

Why This Helps:

Because the mind tends to see transition as erasure. Vectoring restores continuity — reminding you that capability travels, even when roles change.

Examples:

- The discipline that once supported an organization now supports your own boundaries.

- The adaptability you developed under pressure becomes proof that you can learn again.

Overcome — Release the Fear of Being Judged for Starting Again

Career pivots often activate imagined scrutiny.

Say gently:

"No one is tracking my timeline as closely as I am."

Why This Helps:

Because the mind often magnifies the idea that others are watching and evaluating every move. In reality, most people are focused on their own paths. Releasing that imagined audience frees you to begin again without carrying unnecessary shame or pressure.

Examples:

• You let go of the need to explain your departure to everyone.
• You allow yourself to be new at something without narrating it as a downgrade.

Travel Forward — Build the New Without Re-Arguing the Old

At some point, reflection becomes rumination.

Tell yourself:

"I don't need to justify where I've been to begin where I'm going."

Why This Helps:

Because forward motion restores agency.

Examples:

• You stop rehearsing why you left and start shaping what you're building.
• You choose steps that support sustainability, not just familiarity.

Reflection Prompts

• *Which inner rule has kept me equating stability with safety?*

• *What strengths from my previous role are portable — regardless of title?*

• *Where am I rushing for certainty instead of allowing recalibration?*

- *What would forward movement look like if I trusted myself more than my fear?*

Closing Thoughts

Career transitions are not just professional events. They are identity events.

They ask us to loosen old definitions, release borrowed certainty, and trust that who we are is larger than where we work.

Pause.
Introspect.
Vector.
Overcome.
Travel Forward.

That is how work stops controlling your sense of worth and begins to support the life you have.

Chapter 15: P.I.V.O.T.™ for Students

From Graduation to… Now What?

You've done what you were told.
You studied. You graduated. You showed up.

For some, that means sitting at a desk that isn't temporary, holding a role that suddenly feels very real. For others, graduation looks different. You move back home because the job hasn't come yet. The relief of finishing school is quickly replaced by something heavier. All that effort. All that money. And now the unspoken question hangs in the air:

Now what?

That moment can feel deeply unsettling — not because you've failed, but because an identity you lived inside for years has ended, and the next one hasn't fully formed yet.

I remember my own early professional days many moons ago. The late 1990s were certainly a different era, but the experience mirrors what I now see among many new graduates. I had excelled in college in the United States, far away from my home in South Africa. I was confident. I assumed that because I had done everything "right," the working world would open its arms with ease.

It didn't.

I was shocked by how many job applications I sent out, and how many rejections followed. Eventually, I landed a paid internship in Washington, D.C. I arrived expecting myself to be able to contribute deep ideas as I had been trained. I also expected my ideas to be welcomed, just as my professors had done. Instead, I was assigned to the Xerox machine. I was told I was lucky even to have a paid internship, since many graduates were working for free.

That gap — between expectation and reality — is where many students quietly struggle.

You may have done everything right yet still feel unsure of where you fit. The structure and clarity of school disappear, and suddenly the rules feel less visible. Feedback is no longer constant. Progress is harder to measure. You're learning in real time, often without knowing whether you're doing it well.

In that space, it's easy to misread uncertainty as inadequacy. You begin to wonder whether you belong, whether you're ready, whether everyone else somehow received a guidebook you missed. Not because you lack ability, but because the identity you relied on as a student no longer applies in the same way.

Sometimes, all it takes is a simple reframing to shift the weight of that moment. When someone says, *"We don't expect you to know everything. We expect you to learn,"* the pressure eases. Performance gives way to permission. The goal stops being to prove yourself and becomes learning how to stay steady while you learn.

Because stepping into life beyond school isn't just a professional transition.
It's an identity transition.

When Graduation Disrupts Identity

School gives structure. Milestones. Feedback. Clear signals of progress.

Graduation removes much of that overnight.

It often creates a quiet but powerful gap. You expected clarity, confidence, and forward motion. Instead, you find uncertainty, ambiguity, and a constant feeling of being "new." P.I.V.O.T.™ helps you move through that gap without turning uncertainty into self-doubt.

Pause — Don't Rush to Prove Yourself

In the early days of a first job, the instinct is often to perform. To speak quickly. To demonstrate knowledge. To hide what you don't yet understand.
Pause interrupts that pressure.

Say to yourself:

"I don't need to know everything yet. I need to pay attention."

Pause is not about falling behind. It is about giving your mind time to orient before deciding what to do.

Why this helps

Pausing calms the nervous system and reduces overwhelm. It shifts your focus from self-monitoring to sensemaking — from *How am I doing?* to *What is actually happening here?*

Examples

Instead of jumping into conversations to sound capable, you listen for how decisions are made and what truly matters.

- When something feels unfamiliar, you pause before judging yourself and remind yourself that newness is expected.

Introspect — Separate Your Worth from Your Readiness

Many graduates carry an unspoken belief: *I should be ready now.*
Yet the transition from student to professional is not simply about knowledge—it is an identity shift, from being a successful student to becoming a developing professional.

Ask yourself:

"What expectations am I placing on myself that don't match reality?"

Early careers are not about certainty. They are about orientation.

Why This Helps

Introspection loosens the link between confidence and immediate competence. It allows you to anchor your identity in growth rather than mastery.

Examples

- You notice the pressure to appear confident and remind yourself that learning is not a flaw.
- You recognize uncertainty as part of transition, not evidence of inadequacy.

Vector — Use What You Already Know How to Do

New environments can make even capable people feel inexperienced. Vector helps you reconnect with what you already know.

Say to yourself:
"I've learned hard things before. I can learn this too."

You are not starting from nothing. You are building from memory.

Why this helps

Vector restores confidence by reconnecting you with past learning. Trust grows from remembered capability, not external reassurance.

Examples

- You apply the discipline that helped you study for exams to learning systems, tools, or processes at work.
- You notice small progress — understanding one more thing today than yesterday — and let that build momentum.

Overcome — Release the Fear of Being Seen as Inexperienced

Early career transitions often trigger self-consciousness. The fear is not failure — it is exposure.

Say gently:
"I am allowed to learn in public."

Why this helps

Because learning always involves moments of uncertainty. When the fear of being seen as inexperienced softens, the pressure to appear competent fades, making it easier to stay open, curious, and engaged in the learning process.

Examples

- You ask for clarification instead of pretending to understand.
- You allow yourself to make mistakes without turning them into stories about your worth.

Travel Forward — Commit To Moving Forward

There is no moment when everything suddenly clicks. There is only accumulation. Growth happens when you stop looking back to measure what you've lost or where you "should" be, and instead commit to moving forward from where you are.

Tell yourself:

"My job is not to arrive. It is to keep moving and learning."

Why this helps

Traveling forward shifts your focus from comparison and regret to momentum. It helps you release the habit of mentally revisiting the past and redirects your energy toward building experience in the present.

Examples

- You reflect on what you are learning now, rather than replaying what you think you should already know.

- You resist comparing your beginning to someone else's middle and stay anchored in your own forward motion.

Reflection Prompts

- *What fears surface when I think about entering the workplace?*
- *What assumptions am I making about how ready I should be?*
- *What skills or habits from school can I repurpose here?*
- *Where am I confusing uncertainty with inadequacy?*
- *What would it look like to trust myself while I learn?*

Closing Thought

Graduation doesn't mark the end of learning.
It marks the end of certainty.

The world beyond school is less structured, more ambiguous, and constantly changing. That doesn't mean you're unprepared. It means the rules have changed.

When you learn to steady your mind first — to pause, reflect, redirect, soften fear, and move forward — uncertainty stops being something to outrun. It becomes something you know how to navigate.

Pause.
Introspect.
Vector.

Overcome.
Travel Forward.

That is how growth becomes grounded and how you learn to dance with change.

Chapter 16: P.I.V.O.T.™ For Marketers

From Influence to Coherence

Of all the professions I've worked in over the years, marketing holds a special place in my heart. I remember the moment, about ten years ago, when I decided to pivot into the field. At the time, I was working as an international economist for the South African government. It was stable work, and on paper, it mattered. But I was bored—and more than that, I felt disconnected from impact.

I spent my days researching and advising policy, yet I couldn't see how my work changed minds or moved people. I remember telling myself, *"In my next career, I need to be closer to how people actually decide."* Marketing came to mind almost immediately, and slowly, I began to build my way into the profession.

What drew me in was influence—shaping perception, signaling value, and helping people make choices in complex environments.

But for many marketers today, the challenge is no longer influence.

It is **coherence**.

The strategies still work. The dashboards still update. The metrics still move. But the volume of data, platforms, signals, and optimization levers has exploded. Every campaign generates insight. Every insight competes for attention. Every decision can be justified—and questioned—by another dataset.

Marketers are no longer short on information.
They are overwhelmed by it.

This tension shows up in quiet but familiar ways—analysis paralysis. Constant second-guessing. Chasing performance signals that contradict one another. A feeling of reacting rather than deciding. A sense that the work is technically sophisticated, yet mentally exhausting.

This is not because marketers have lost their skills.
It is because the marketing context has become saturated.

Today's marketers operate inside a continuous stream of data, testing cycles, real-time feedback, and algorithmic pressure. Speed is rewarded. Certainty is expected. Yet the ground keeps shifting.

Audiences fragment and grow more skeptical. Platforms change. Signals decay faster than they can be interpreted. Trust is harder to earn.

When that happens, it's not just strategy that gets disrupted.
Its orientation.

And when orientation is lost, identity follows.

Many marketers find themselves caught between what the data suggests and what actually makes sense. Between reacting to signals and trusting their judgment. Between optimization and meaning.

This is where P.I.V.O.T.™ becomes useful—not as a marketing framework or decision model, but as a mental recalibration—a way for marketers to restore coherence in their own thinking while working inside constant disruption and volatility.

When Marketing Disrupts Orientation

Marketing roles often reward speed, confidence, and decisiveness. You are expected to know what will work, what will convert, and what to test next. But when inputs multiply faster than understanding can keep pace, clarity erodes.

Marketers may begin to question:

- *Which signals actually matter?*
- *Am I responding to insight—or noise?*
- *Do I trust the data, or my judgment?*
- *Why does everything feel urgent, yet unclear?*

These questions are rarely spoken aloud. Instead, they show up as overwork, indecision, cynicism, or detachment—not because marketers lack expertise, but because their **mental field has become overcrowded**.

Before a strategy can be clarified, the **inner response must settle**.

That is the work of P.I.V.O.T.™.

Below are some suggestions on how the individual marketer might use this framework to gain more internal anchoring amid the very fast-paced, data-saturated marketing world.

P.I.V.O.T.™ Application

Restoring Coherence in a Saturated Marketing Environment

Pause — Interrupt the Urge to Push

In high-performance marketing environments, motion often replaces reflection. Dashboards refresh. Alerts trigger—results dip or spike. Launching, optimizing, testing, and repeating can become a way to avoid confronting discomfort about direction. Pausing can feel risky because it interrupts momentum — but it is often the only way to notice misalignment before it hardens.

So, interrupt the urge to act. Do nothing for a few minutes.

Say to yourself:
"Before I respond to the data, I just need to re-center my thinking."

Why This Helps

Pause interrupts reactivity. It prevents marketers from confusing urgency with insight and restores choice in how information is interpreted.

Examples

- Instead of immediately adjusting a campaign, you pause to ask what actually changed—and what did not.
- You notice whether pressure is coming from the data itself or from expectations layered onto it.

Saturation does not just overload systems; it strains the marketer's **sense of judgment and self-trust**. Over time, constant signals, shifting metrics, and external pressure don't just confuse decisions—they quietly distort how marketers see themselves in their work.

Introspection is the moment you turn inward and ask not only *what is happening*, but *what it is doing to you.*

Ask yourself:
"Where has my decision-making become reactive instead of intentional?"
"What part of my professional identity feels under pressure to perform, prove, or keep up?"

Why This Helps

Introspection reveals how external complexity affects internal clarity and identity. It reframes fatigue not as incompetence, but as a signal that something meaningful has slipped out of alignment.

When identity is strained—when confidence becomes conditional on metrics, certainty, or speed—judgment suffers. Introspection restores orientation by helping marketers separate who they are from the noise they navigate.

Examples

- You recognize that conflicting metrics are eroding your **confidence**, not your capability.
- You notice when optimization has replaced **intention**, and performance has begun to stand in for judgment.
- You acknowledge the pressure to appear certain—even when the picture is incomplete—and how that pressure is reshaping how you show up in your role.

Vector — Re-Aim Existing Insight Toward Coherence

In saturation, the temptation is to add more tools, more data, more tests. Vector reminds you that clarity rarely comes from expanding inputs. It comes from trusting your ability to *learn your way forward* using what you already know.

Vector is not about having the right answer in advance. It is about restoring confidence in your capacity to interpret, adjust, and re-aim as conditions change.

Say to yourself:
"I don't need more information. I need a clearer direction."
"I already can learn what this moment requires."

Why This Helps

Vector restores agency by reconnecting insight with self-trust. It shifts the inner dialogue from *keeping up* to *making sense*. When marketers trust their ability to learn amid uncertainty and complexity, complexity becomes navigable rather than paralyzing.

Instead of reacting to every signal, Vector helps you choose which signals deserve weight—and reminds you that judgment improves through engagement, not perfection.

Examples

- You prioritize a small set of metrics aligned with intent, trusting that you can refine them as understanding deepens.
- You use research to **learn**, not just to optimize—clarifying audience meaning rather than chasing clicks.
- You align teams around interpretation, not just reporting, reinforcing shared learning instead of performative certainty.

Overcome — Release the Need for Perfect Certainty

Saturated environments reward the *appearance* of certainty. But when clarity is always partial, and conditions keep shifting, mistakes happen, and waiting to feel fully sure often becomes its own form of paralysis.

What often causes the greatest strain is not the mistake itself, but what happens around it: *the fear of being wrong* and the tendency to *punish ourselves afterward.*

Marketers delay decisions, waiting for perfect clarity, afraid of making a visible misstep. At the same time, they replay past choices—second-guessing timing, interpreting outcomes as personal failure, and carrying forward the weight of decisions made with incomplete information.

Overcoming is the moment you stop fighting yourself—both before and after action.

Say gently to yourself:
"I can decide responsibly without knowing everything."
"I made the best decision I could with what I knew then."

Why This Helps

Overcome loosens the grip of self-judgment. It separates accountability from self-punishment and releases energy trapped in fear and hindsight.

When past decisions are no longer used as evidence against your competence and future decisions no longer require perfect certainty, movement becomes possible again.

Progress does not arrive all at once in volatile environments. It often shows up in small adjustments, clearer interpretations, or quieter confidence. Allowing those small wins to count restores trust in your judgment and rebuilds momentum without demanding perfection.

Examples

- You make principled decisions based on directional insight rather than waiting for exhaustive proof.
- You acknowledge when an outcome fell short without turning it into a personal verdict.
- You notice small improvements in clarity, alignment, or learning—and allow them to matter.
- You stop equating confidence with accuracy, and instead trust your ability to adjust as understanding evolves.

Travel Forward — Practice Coherence in Motion

Coherence is not a fixed state. It is something you practice while conditions continue to change.

Tell yourself:
"I can move forward while clarity continues to form."

Why This Helps

Travel Forward prevents stagnation. It reframes marketing as adaptive sensemaking rather than a constant reaction.

Examples

- You build campaigns that prioritize understanding over volume.
- You revisit assumptions regularly without destabilizing direction.
- You allow strategies to evolve without abandoning coherence.

Reflection Prompts

- *Where has data begun to overwhelm judgment?*
- *Which signals deserve less weight right now?*
- *What would clarity look like—not more information, but better orientation?*
- *Where am I reacting instead of choosing?*
- *How can coherence guide my next decision?*

Closing Thought

Marketing is no longer constrained by information.
It is constrained by **attention and meaning**.

In saturated environments, the marketer's greatest asset is not more data, but a steady mind. When you pause, reflect, redirect, soften fear, and move forward deliberately, marketing becomes less about chasing signals and more about creating sense.

Pause.
Introspect.
Vector.
Overcome.
Travel Forward.

That is how marketing adapts—
with coherence intact.

Chapter 17: P.I.V.O.T.™ for Leaders

From Managing Change to Holding Meaning

The email arrives late in the evening, long after the day's meetings have ended. Another update. Another shift in direction. Another decision that will disappoint someone, no matter how carefully it is made.

The leader closes the laptop and exhales. Tomorrow, they will need to explain why priorities have changed again, why resources are being redirected. Why does the plan that everyone agreed on three months ago no longer apply?

They are not afraid of the work. They are afraid of what this constant recalibration is doing to their people — and to themselves.

They wonder, quietly, when leadership became less about knowing what to do and more about carrying what cannot be fixed.

Meanwhile, teams feel it. People quit. Companies lose their best talent, and productivity bleeds.

A leader I interviewed in higher education once shared how a highly capable employee chose to leave during a merger—not because the new role lacked opportunity, but because they could not reconcile reporting to someone they perceived as junior. The loss had little to do with skill or growth and everything to do with identity.

Leadership in an Age of Relentless Change

An industry leader I interviewed shared how fear of failure among leaders has become one of the most significant threats to business success. He described how senior and middle managers cost his ventures millions to competitors — not because they lacked intelligence or opportunity, but because they could not take the necessary risks to grow the business.

"The higher up the ladder in the company," he explained, "the more intense the fear of change — because there is simply more to lose if things don't go well."

What this reveals is not poor leadership, but **unprocessed meaning loss**. When identity, status, and self-worth become tightly coupled to outcomes, leaders default to protection rather than possibility. Fear does not stop change — it simply turns possibility into self-protection.

Let's take a closer look at what weighs so heavily on leaders.

What Leaders Are Actually Carrying

In nonprofit and public-service settings, change often shows up not as a single dramatic event, but as a series of layered, compounding shifts. A refinancing. A merger. A new legal structure. A system rebuild. An audit cycle that no longer fits neatly into the calendar.

What looks on paper like an operational decision becomes, in practice, hundreds of small moments of uncertainty:
Which entity does this invoice belong to? Which ledger should this be coded under? Which button do I click now? What happens if I get this wrong?

This is not resistance. It is cognitive and emotional load.

In one small nonprofit organization serving low-income older adults, a restructuring collapsed multiple entities into a single one, according to a leader I interviewed. Accounting and occupancy systems had to be rebuilt. Reporting rules changed. Even front-desk staff had to relearn how to enter work orders so costs would land in the correct place.

No one objected to the change. But people hesitated. They double-checked. They asked again. They worried about making mistakes that could ripple into audits or compliance issues. Confusion, not defiance, slowed progress.

Layered onto this were human transitions. A long-tenured employee retired, taking with her decades of institutional knowledge. Her successor brought fresh eyes, carefully studying regulations and uncovering more efficient ways of working. Compliance had never been the issue — habit was. The phrase *"we've always done it this way"* quietly revealed where learning had stalled.

Across contexts, the pattern is consistent. Resistance is not stubbornness. It is sensemaking strain. Conflict is not interpersonal failure. It is unprocessed meaning loss. Burnout is not a weakness. It is prolonged inner resistance.

Leaders are not only managing systems. They are holding the emotional weight of people trying not to get it wrong.

Why Traditional Change Approaches Fall Short

Most leadership development prepares people to manage tasks, processes, and outcomes. Very little prepares them to manage the inner experience of change — their own or others'.

When leaders themselves are overwhelmed, the instinct is to push through. Urgency replaces clarity. Speed replaces sensemaking. Control replaces presence.

The leadership coach I interviewed also shared that, in many environments, leadership has quietly been redefined. Where service and care were once understood as strengths, leaders are now rewarded for decisiveness, endurance, and emotional containment. Strength becomes synonymous with suppression.

Under these conditions, leaders override their own internal signals. They push forward not because it is wise, but because it is sanctioned. Mixed messages emerge. Implementation dates blur. People receive different answers from different leaders. Anxiety grows, not because change is wrong, but because meaning is unstable.

What is missing is not strategy. What is missing is a way to steady and reorient the mind as leaders navigate change so they can move with clarity rather than reaction.

This is the role of P.I.V.O.T.™.

P.I.V.O.T.™ as a Leadership Sensemaking Tool

Recalibrating the Leader First — So Change Can Be Held

P.I.V.O.T.™ is not a performance framework. It is a **mental recalibration process** leaders can use when change disrupts meaning, identity, and orientation.

Leadership during change is not only about how leaders regulate themselves. It is about how their internal steadiness shapes the environments in which others must make sense of what is happening.

When leaders practice P.I.V.O.T.™ internally, they naturally extend it outward—designing conditions that reduce fear, preserve dignity, and support forward motion without coercion.

PAUSE — Interrupt Reactivity Before Decisions Harden

Change often arrives with urgency. PAUSE invites leaders to interrupt momentum long enough for meaning to catch up.

This is not about delaying decisions. It is about preventing fear-driven action from masquerading as leadership.

Tell yourself:

I don't need an immediate resolution to lead well.

Why This Helps

Pausing stabilizes the leader's nervous system and restores choice. It prevents urgency from being mistaken for clarity and allows leaders to respond rather than react. When leaders slow down internally, teams sense that steadiness and are less likely to scramble.

How This Shows Up in Practice

- Leadership voices align before decisions are announced, reducing confusion.

- Changes are sequenced deliberately instead of layered chaotically.

- Uncertainty is named honestly before action is requested.
- PAUSE is not inactivity. It is containment.

INTROSPECT — Name Identity Impact, Not Just Structural Change

Most resistance is not to the work itself. It is what the change implies about competence, status, or belonging.

A leader I interviewed in higher education shared how a highly capable employee chose to leave during a merger—not because the new role lacked opportunity, but because they could not reconcile reporting to someone they perceived as junior. The loss had little to do with skill or growth and everything to do with identity. When identity impact goes unnamed, leaders often misread departure as resistance, when it is actually grief for a self that no longer fits.

Moments like these ask something different of leaders. Not more explanation or persuasion, but the willingness to recognize what the change is touching beneath the surface.

Tell yourself:

This change affects identity, not just structure.

Why This Helps

Introspect helps leaders notice how change is experienced internally by themselves and by others. When identity impact goes unnamed, people protect themselves by hesitating or withdrawing. Naming it reduces fear and restores self-trust.

For leaders, INTROSPECT is ethical preparation. Before leading others, leaders must be clear about who they are becoming under pressure, what they value, and what they are unwilling to trade for speed or approval.

VECTOR — Restore Confidence in Learning, Not Replacement

Leaders sometimes communicate—without intending to—that the past no longer matters. Yet experience can help anchor people as they navigate change.

VECTOR restores continuity by reminding people that their ability to learn and adapt has not disappeared.

This step is internal before it is structural.

Tell yourself:

We are building on what already exists.

Why This Helps

Vector restores confidence—both the leader's and the team's—in the ability to learn on the move. When people trust that their experience still matters, change becomes navigable rather than threatening.

OVERCOME — Release Fear and Self-Judgment Around Imperfection

Fear of mistakes quietly shuts down adaptability. Leaders feel it before anyone else —fear of being wrong, of mis-stepping publicly, of carrying responsibility for outcomes shaped by incomplete information.

Over time, leaders also carry self-judgment for past decisions, replaying what could have gone differently.

Tell yourself:

Mistakes are part of learning, not evidence of failure.

Why This Helps

Overcome separates accountability from self-punishment. When leaders release fear and soften judgment—both about the future and the past—energy returns. Teams remain engaged instead of defensive. Psychological safety becomes a byproduct of inner steadiness, not a technique.

TRAVEL FORWARD — Commit to Meaningful Motion Without Re-Litigation

Leaders and teams struggle to move forward when the past remains emotionally unresolved. Travel Forward is the commitment to proceed without dragging old decisions along.

Tell yourself:
Forward movement requires shared meaning, not perfect certainty.

Why This Helps

Travel Forward redirects attention from rumination to orientation. It frames leadership as ongoing sensemaking rather than constant explanation or control. Meaning gives people something to move toward—not just something to leave behind.

When P.I.V.O.T.™ Is Already at Work

What stands out in the leader interview is not novelty, but recognition. P.I.V.O.T.™ names what grounded leaders are already doing intuitively—slowing reaction, naming identity impact, trusting learning, releasing perfection, and sustaining forward motion.

The difference is not enthusiasm for change.
It is an **orientation within it**.

Closing Reflection

When leaders extend P.I.V.O.T.™ beyond themselves, change becomes something people can participate in—not just endure.

- **PAUSE** stabilizes reactivity
- **INTROSPECT** preserves dignity
- **VECTOR** restores learning confidence
- **OVERCOME** frees energy trapped in fear
- **TRAVEL FORWARD** sustains meaning in motion

This is not about controlling change.
It is about steering change in ways the human mind can make sense of and hold onto.

And that is how leaders and teams move forward—together.

Chapter 18: P.I.V.O.T.™ for People Leaders (OD & HR)

Holding Meaning In The Middle

Decades of research tell a consistent story: most organizational change efforts struggle to deliver on their promises. *Harvard Business Review* reported as early as 2000 that nearly 70 percent of change initiatives fail. In the era of artificial intelligence, the challenge has only intensified. While McKinsey reports that nearly 80 percent of organizations now use generative AI, very few achieve meaningful, enterprise-wide transformation.

What these numbers often overlook is where the real strain of change is carried.

Within organizations, those closest to people—human resource professionals, organizational development leaders, and culture stewards—often shoulder the heaviest weight. They are asked to steady others while navigating disruption themselves. To translate executive decisions into human impact. To preserve clarity, morale, and trust while structures shift and familiar ways of working dissolve.

Much of this work happens quietly.

Titles change. Teams are reorganized. Reporting lines shift. Priorities are redefined. Sometimes change is strategic and intentional. Other times, it is reactive, driven by pressure or uncertainty. Either way, the impact lands on people—and on the professionals responsible for guiding them through it.

This work matters deeply.

And it carries an invisible tension.

When it comes to teams, processes may be sound. Communication plans may be thorough. Timelines may be clear. And yet, beneath the surface, something often feels unsettled. Resistance lingers. Fatigue grows. Trust these. Engagement becomes harder to sustain.

This is not a failure of planning.

It is a signal that meaning has been disrupted.

Organizational change does more than alter workflows or structures. It interrupts identity. It disrupts how people understand their roles, their value, and their place within the system. When meaning is disrupted, fear and resistance naturally follow.

HR and OD professionals often find themselves caught in the middle between strategy and humanity. Between what must change and what people are still grieving.

People leaders do not just implement change.
They absorb its emotional impact.

This is where **P.I.V.O.T.™** becomes useful—not as another engagement tool or organizational change model, but as a mental recalibration for the people leader. A way to stabilize one's own inner response during disruption, so that leadership presence, judgment, and choice remain intact.

P.I.V.O.T.™ does not promise to remove fear, eliminate resistance, or empower everyone through change. Instead, it helps people leaders reduce fear within themselves, regain a sense of internal steadiness, and respond deliberately rather than reactively while holding the center of the system.

When Organizational Change Disrupts Identity

Organizational change often asks people to adapt before they have had time to understand what they are losing.

Teams may hear messages like:
This is necessary.
This will make us stronger.
This is the new direction.

But beneath those messages are quieter, more personal questions:

- Who am I now in this organization?
- Do I still belong here?
- Does my work still matter?
- Can I trust what comes next?

Leaders are not immune to these questions. In fact, they often carry them silently while helping others navigate the same uncertainty.

When identity disruption goes unacknowledged, it shows up as resistance, disengagement, cynicism, or compliance without commitment—not because people are difficult, but because their inner bearings have been shaken.

Before culture can stabilize, the leader's inner response must settle.

That is the primary work of P.I.V.O.T.™.

One industry leader I interviewed described organizational change as having two sides: the *transmission side*, where leaders design systems, decisions, and communication, and the *reception side*, where people must internally receive and make sense of what is being asked of them.

Most organizations invest heavily in transmission. Far less attention is paid to equipping leaders and their teams to absorb change internally without fear or overwhelm.

P.I.V.O.T.™ addresses that gap by first stabilizing the people leader's mind, creating the conditions for steadier leadership and clearer relational dynamics during change.

What follows shows how P.I.V.O.T.™ supports people leaders—and how that steadiness can be *offered* rather than imposed to individual team members.

P.I.V.O.T.™ Application

Restoring Internal Stability During Organizational Change

P.I.V.O.T.™ for the People Leader

Pause — Interrupt the Rush to Fix

During organizational change, urgency often replaces presence. There is pressure to communicate quickly, reassure constantly, and resolve resistance immediately. Pausing can feel irresponsible when anxiety is high—yet it is often the only way to respond wisely.

Say to yourself:
"Before I try to steady others, I need to steady myself."

Why this helps

Pause interrupts emotional contagion. It prevents people leaders from absorbing collective anxiety and reacting automatically instead of responding with clarity.

Examples

- Before responding to pushback, you notice whether you are trying to calm others—or calm yourself.
- Instead of rushing to justify the change, you create space to understand what meaning is being disrupted.

Introspect — Acknowledge the Identity Shift at Play

Resistance to change is rarely about the change itself. It is about what the change threatens—belonging, competence, status, or purpose.

Ask yourself:

"What identities are being disrupted here—including my own?"

Why this helps

when leaders recognize that resistance often reflects an identity disruption rather than simple opposition, they can respond with curiosity and clarity instead of defensiveness.

Examples

- You recognize that a team's resistance reflects loss of mastery, not unwillingness.
- You notice your own strain when positioned as the messenger rather than the decision-maker.
- You acknowledge the tension of holding organizational loyalty and human empathy at the same time.

Vector — Reconnect to the Capacity to Learn in Motion

In moments of disruption, there is pressure to add more—more initiatives, more messaging, more frameworks—to compensate for uncertainty. But overwhelm rarely signals a lack of tools. More often, it reflects a loss of confidence in one's ability to learn while moving.

Vector reminds people leaders that they are not starting from zero. Even when roles shift and familiar reference points dissolve, the capacity to learn has not disappeared.

Say to yourself:

"I already know how to learn through uncertainty. I can use what I know to find my footing again."

Why this helps

Vector restores confidence in the ability to learn. When leaders remember they are not starting from zero, the pressure to immediately master the future softens, making it easier to move forward step by step.

Examples

- You draw on past experiences of ambiguity—previous reorganizations, role shifts, or moments of uncertainty—to remind yourself: *I've learned my way through change before.*

- You notice transferable strengths (sensemaking, listening, translating complexity) and consciously rely on them while the new structure takes shape.

- Instead of introducing new initiatives to "fix" discomfort, you use familiar spaces—meetings, check-ins, conversations—as places to practice learning together in real time.

Overcome — Release the Need to Get Change 'Right'

People leaders often carry an unspoken fear: *If people struggle, I've failed.*

Say gently:

"I don't need to remove discomfort to support people through it."

Why this helps

Overcome softens the fear of judgment that drives over-functioning. It allows leaders to hold space without absorbing responsibility for every emotional response.

Examples

- You stop trying to convince people that change is positive before they are ready.
- You allow mixed reactions without rushing to resolve them.
- You trust that discomfort does not mean harm—it means transition.

Travel Forward — Commit to Meaning While Letting Go of the Past

Organizational change is rarely linear. Meaning is rebuilt gradually, through consistency rather than certainty. But forward movement requires more than patience; it requires a conscious decision to stop anchoring the present to what used to be.

Travel Forward is the moment where leaders release the mental habit of replaying old structures, old roles, or old measures of success—and choose to lead from where they are now.

Tell yourself:
"I don't need to resolve the past to move forward. I can lead in motion, even while clarity is still forming."

Why this helps

Travel Forward prevents stagnation by redirecting energy away from lament and toward creation. It restores agency by shifting focus from what was lost or disrupted to what is actively being built. Leadership becomes less about defending yesterday and more about orienting people toward what is emerging.

Examples

- You stop revisiting how things *should* have been handled and focus instead on what needs attention now.
- You reinforce small moments of trust instead of waiting for full buy-in.
- You allow teams to redefine success as they adapt, rather than forcing old metrics onto new realities.
- You model forward commitment by speaking in terms of *next steps* rather than *what used to work.*

P.I.V.O.T.™ for the Individual Team Member

Steadying the leader's mind is one thing. Translating that steadiness to teams is another.

People leaders are not only holding space; they can actively **equip individuals** with language and inner anchors that reduce resistance before it hardens.

This is not about coaching everyone through change. It is about offering a simple, human mental map that helps people regain their footing.

Pause — Create a Moment Before Reaction

Invite team members to notice the moment fear shows up.

Offer language like:

"Before reacting to this change, let's take a breath and notice what's coming up."

Why this helps

Pause interrupts the automatic stress response. It separates discomfort from danger and gives the nervous system a chance to settle.

Example

A team member recognizes their anxiety before interpreting it as a signal that something is wrong.

Introspect — Name What Feels Threatened

Help individuals reflect on what the change is touching internally.

Ask:

"What feels at risk for you right now — your role, your expertise, your sense of stability?"

Why this helps

Naming the identity impact reduces confusion and self-judgment. It reframes fear as information rather than weakness.

Example

A high performer realizes that their resistance is tied to a loss of mastery, not to opposition to progress.

Vector — Reconnect to What Still Transfers

Guide people to recognize what they already bring forward.

Say:

"What skills or strengths still apply here, even if the context is changing?"

Why this helps

Vectoring restores agency by reminding people that change does not erase capability.

Example

An employee sees how their problem-solving skills remain valuable, even as tools evolve.

Overcome — Normalize Imperfect Transition

Permit learning curves.

Reassure:

"Not having it figured out yet doesn't mean you're failing."

Why this helps

This softens self-judgment and reduces the shame that often fuels quiet disengagement.

Example

A team member stays engaged instead of withdrawing when early attempts feel clumsy.

Travel Forward — Focus on the Next Meaningful Step

Encourage forward motion without forcing certainty.

Invite:

"What is one small step you can take while clarity continues to form?"

Why this helps

Traveling forward prevents paralysis. It allows people to participate in change without needing a full resolution first.

Example

Someone experiments, learns, and adapts rather than waiting to feel ready.

Reflection Prompts

- *Where might this change be disrupting identity, not just structure?*
- *What pressure am I carrying that isn't mine to hold alone?*
- *How can I support meaning before asking for commitment?*
- *Where might listening be more stabilizing than explaining?*
- *What does steady leadership look like right now?*

Closing Thought

Organizational change is not just a strategic exercise.

It is a human experience.

HR and OD professionals are not only managing systems — they are holding meaning during moments of uncertainty. When you steady your inner response first — when you pause, reflect, redirect, soften fear, and move forward — you create the conditions for people to adapt without losing themselves.

Pause.
Introspect.
Vector.
Overcome.
Travel Forward.

That is how people leaders and their teams move through disruption — with clarity, dignity, and trust intact - while the playbook keeps changing.

PART III: P.I.V.O.T™ in Systems

Chapter 19: When Technology Disrupts Meaning

Applying P.I.V.O.T.™ in the Age of AI

Technology has always changed how we live and work. What feels different now is not the change itself. It is the speed, scale, and intimacy with which change is arriving.

Artificial intelligence is not only altering tasks and workflows. It is quietly reshaping how people understand their value, relevance, and place in the world. It challenges long-held assumptions about expertise, effort, creativity, and even intelligence, and it does so faster than the mind can comfortably integrate.

This is why AI disruption often feels unsettling before it feels practical.

For many, the discomfort shows up as anxiety about being replaced, falling behind, or no longer being needed For others, it appears as resistance, dismissal, or overconfidence — attempts to minimize the impact in order to preserve a sense of stability. Some feel excitement mixed with unease. Others feel frozen, unsure where to begin.

These reactions are often labeled as fear of technology or resistance to change.

But that is not what is happening.

What AI disrupts first is meaning.

It unsettles the inner story people rely on to answer quiet but essential questions:
What am I good at?
Where do I add value?
Who am I in this new landscape?

When those answers wobble, fear is a natural byproduct — not a flaw.

This chapter is not about learning AI tools, predicting the future, or keeping up with technological trends. It is about understanding *why* AI feels destabilizing and *how* to steady yourself — or those you lead — before fear takes the wheel.

This is where P.I.V.O.T.™ becomes especially relevant. It equips the human psyche in the face of AI.

When Technology Outpaces Meaning

Unlike earlier waves of technological change, AI touches work that has traditionally been tied to identity: thinking, writing, analyzing, creating, deciding. Tasks that once signaled competence or expertise can now be automated or assisted in seconds.

This creates a subtle but profound inner disruption.

What makes AI different is not only *what* it changes, but **where it lands** — directly on how people understand their value, relevance, and place in the system.

One HR leader I interviewed described this disruption from the front lines. As the person responsible for the human side of AI-driven transition, she found herself absorbing multiple shocks at once:

- Intergenerational differences in how teams responded to AI
- Inertia rooted in long-standing habits: *"this is how we've always done things."*
- Fear that AI would replace people's jobs
- The absence of clear guardrails to accompany AI training and rollout

What she was describing was not resistance to technology.

It was a disorientation of meaning.

People are not just asking, *"Can I learn this?"*
They are asking, *"Do I still matter?"*

When meaning collapses faster than it can be rebuilt, the nervous system responds. Comparison increases. Self-doubt grows. Performance pressure tightens. Some rush to prove relevance; others withdraw to protect dignity.

These are not signs of weakness.
They are signs that the mind is searching for orientation.

Before adaptability can emerge, the inner self must recalibrate.

That is the work of P.I.V.O.T.™. It can help individuals anchor and empower themselves amidst AI-induced disruptions without doing anything external.

P.I.V.O.T.™ Application
Using AI disruption as an illustration of a broader inner recalibration

Pause — Don't Let Speed Decide the Story

"I don't need to decide what this means or react yet."

Introspect — Notice What This Is Stirring About Who You Are

"What part of my identity feels challenged right now?"

Vector — Use What You Already Know How to Do

"I have learned hard things before. I can learn this too."

Overcome — Release the Pressure to Master This Perfectly

"I am allowed to be new at this."

Travel Forward — Engage Without Over-Identifying

"I don't need to know where this leads to take the next step."

Why This Helps in the Age of AI

AI accelerates disruption, but it does not change the human mechanism underneath it.

When meaning steadies, fear eases.
When fear eases, learning becomes possible.
When learning becomes possible, adaptability follows.

P.I.V.O.T.™ does not make AI less powerful.
It makes people less destabilized by it.

Reflection Prompts

• *What assumptions am I making about what AI means for my value or relevance?*
• *Where am I confusing uncertainty with inadequacy?*
• *Which parts of my identity feel most unsettled right now?*
• *What strengths or ways of learning can I repurpose here?*

• *What would it look like to stay engaged without rushing to define the outcome?*

Closing Thought

AI will continue to change how work is done.
It will not change the fact that humans need meaning before movement.

When you steady your inner response first — before fear hardens into story — disruption becomes something you can meet rather than outrun.

Pause.
Introspect.
Vector.
Overcome.
Travel Forward.

That is how orientation returns — even when the future is still forming.

Chapter 20: How to P.I.V.O.T™ Toward Inclusiveness

Dancing with differences

Inclusiveness is deeply personal to me.

I grew up under institutionalized racism and within a patriarchal society. Long before I had language for social justice—or even spoke fluent English—I called myself a feminist. It was not an academic stance. It was an instinctive refusal to accept the limits being placed on me as a Black girl in South Africa.

Years later, when I arrived in the United States as a college student, I was surprised by how differently diversity was discussed. On the surface, the society appeared progressive. Yet I struggled to understand the depth of frustration I encountered. I was suddenly described as Black, female, and oppressed—while internally, I did not experience myself that way. Nothing I had encountered in the U.S. felt more restrictive than the system I had grown up within.

That dissonance stayed with me.

Over time, I came to understand something essential: difference is not experienced in the abstract. It is experienced through context and meaning.

Differences may show up as race, religion, gender, sexuality, culture, values, politics or worldview. But regardless of its form, it often triggers the same internal response.

Uncertainty.

And like change, uncertainty can feel threatening—not because difference is dangerous, but because it disrupts our internal sense of normal, belonging, or orientation.

In that sense, Dancing with Differences is inseparable from Dancing with Change.

When Difference Disrupts Meaning

When we encounter differences without inner grounding, the mind often reacts before understanding has time to form. We brace. We defend. We withdraw. Or we rush to explain.

Not because we are unkind or intolerant, but because **meaning has been unsettled**.

Whether you experience difference as marginalization or as discomfort, the internal mechanism is similar: the loss of a familiar interpretive frame. And when meaning collapses, fear tends to fill the gap.

This is where P.I.V.O.T.™ becomes useful. It serves not as a moral directive, but as a way to restore internal steadiness before fear hardens into judgment, resentment, or avoidance.

A Personal Moment of Difference

In my mid-twenties, I lived in a rural village in Thailand for over a year. When I arrived, I noticed immediately that no one shared my skin tone. That alone did not unsettle me. By then, I had lived in multiple countries and was accustomed to being visibly different.

What caught me off guard came later.

As I rode my bicycle through the village, children began running behind me, shouting "monkey, monkey" in broken English. At first, I wasn't sure I was hearing correctly. But after repeated encounters and confirmation from other expatriates, I understood.

I was faced with a choice.

I could interpret their behavior as hateful and carry anger and hurt. Or I could consider another possibility: these children had never seen someone with skin as dark as mine. They were trying clumsily and imperfectly to make sense of something unfamiliar using the only reference point they had.

I chose the second interpretation.

That choice did not excuse the children's behavior. But it completely changed my internal experience of it. Instead of carrying resentment, I felt steady. I began engaging with the children—explaining my skin, my hair, my background. Curiosity replaced fear on both sides.

What that experience taught me was this: when meaning collapses, the mind fills the gap—often imperfectly.

And while we cannot control how others respond to difference or us, we can choose how we orient ourselves internally.

That is the heart of P.I.V.O.T.™ in moments of difference.

Applying P.I.V.O.T.™ When Difference Marginalizes You

When difference shows up as exclusion, dismissal, or a threat to your legitimacy, the nervous system often reacts before the mind has time to assess what is happening.

Pause — Do Nothing First

Before concluding that harm is intentional or defined, pause. This is not about denying lived experience or minimizing impact. It is about stabilizing yourself before fear takes over the narrative.

Why this helps

Pause interrupts emotional escalation. It creates space between experience and interpretation.

Introspect — Anchor in Identity

Difference does not diminish worth. It does not invalidate belonging.

Remind yourself:
This moment does not define who I am.

Why this helps

Introspection restores internal reference points when external validation feels uncertain.

Vector — Choose an Interpretation That Preserves Agency

Ask yourself:

What understanding allows me to remain grounded and oriented, rather than reactive or diminished?

When motives are unclear, the mind often fills the gap with the most threatening interpretation. A stabilizing alternative is to consider simpler explanations—unfamiliarity, ignorance, or fear—especially when clear evidence of harm is absent.

If certainty is not available, choose the interpretation that allows you to remain steady and psychologically anchored.

Why This Helps

Vector restores agency by protecting orientation. When people interpret events in ways that preserve their sense of direction and capability, they remain able to respond thoughtfully rather than react defensively.

Overcome — Release the Fear of Being Judged for Responding Imperfectly

When navigating difference, especially from a marginalized position, responses can feel heavily scrutinized. There may be pressure to react calmly, educate others, or represent your group perfectly.

Say to yourself:
"I do not have to handle this moment perfectly in order to deserve respect."

Why This Helps

Overcome softens the fear of being judged for responding imperfectly. Releasing the pressure to represent or respond flawlessly allows people to remain grounded in their dignity rather than becoming trapped in self-monitoring or silence.

Travel Forward — Protect Your Energy

Not every moment of misunderstanding needs to be resolved in real time. Move forward with dignity and self-respect, recognizing that your well-being does not depend on convincing everyone around you.

Why This Helps

Travel Forward redirects attention away from replaying the moment and toward reclaiming your own direction. When people stop investing energy in proving their worth, they regain the freedom to move forward on their own terms.

Applying P.I.V.O.T.™ When Difference Makes You Uncomfortable

Differences can also unsettle those who see themselves as open-minded or well-intentioned. The fear here is often quieter—but just as powerful.

Fear of saying the wrong thing.
Fear of being judged.
Fear of being exposed as inadequate.

Pause — Stay with Discomfort

Notice the urge to withdraw, over-explain, or stay silent. Discomfort is not danger.

Why this helps

Pause prevents fear from masquerading as politeness or distance.

Introspect — Examine the Inner Threat

Ask yourself:
What feels at risk for me right now—my image, my certainty, my sense of being "good"?

Why this helps

Introspection reveals that discomfort often stems from identity threat, not the other person.

Vector — Orient Toward Curiosity

When you're unsure what to say, remember: everyone is human first. You've navigated human connection before. Trust that.

When in doubt, remember this: everyone is human first. You have successfully encountered humans before. You already know how to listen, ask respectfully, and engage with care. Those same instincts apply when learning about different cultures, identities, or worldviews.

You are not starting from zero.

Why this helps

Vector reminds you that you already have what it takes to stay engaged in the face of uncertainty. Instead of retreating because you fear getting it wrong, you lean into the discomfort of not knowing—trusting your existing capacity for human connection to guide learning in motion.

Overcome — Let Go of Perfection

The fear of offending is real especially when we care deeply about others and genuinely want them to feel welcome and respected. That fear can make us hesitate, overthink, or withdraw entirely.

But learning anything new involves missteps.

Mistakes are not a moral failure; they are part of the learning process. Even when a moment feels awkward or uncomfortable, it is rarely permanent. Most missteps are not etched into history—they are moments that can be acknowledged, repaired, and released.

Apologize when needed. Learn from the experience. Then allow yourself to move on.

Why this helps

Overcoming softens the fear of judgment and prevents self-punishment from interrupting learning. It allows curiosity and engagement to continue, even when things don't go perfectly.

True inclusiveness grows through lived relationships, not performance. Commit to engaging differences without needing certainty, control, or immediate resolution.

Why This Helps

Travel Forward turns inclusion from an abstract ideal into an ongoing practice. By staying engaged across differences—even without full clarity—people create space for understanding to develop over time.

A Closing Thought

Dancing with differences, like dancing with change, is not about mastery or certainty. It is about remaining internally steady when meaning is disrupted and choosing orientation and agency rather than fear as uncertainty unfolds.

Inclusiveness begins inside.
With awareness.
With humility.
With the willingness to stay present when difference unsettles what feels familiar.

When we allow others to be different, something subtle but powerful happens.
We make room for ourselves to be different, too.

That is how we dance with differences—not perfectly, but deliberately toward a more inclusive and harmonious world.

Full Circle: Remembering Where the Dance Begins

We've journeyed through the dance of change—from personal awakenings to professional reinventions, from students finding their footing to leaders rediscovering authenticity amidst upheaval. And like every meaningful dance, the ending leads us back to the beginning.

Change isn't a straight line; it's a rhythm. And rhythm always brings us home back to humility, back to curiosity, back to the place where learning begins.

As you close this book, I invite you to remember not just what you've learned, but who you were when you first began learning. Much of what you've read here isn't new. It's built on the shared human experience we all carry and often forget under pressure.

I hope that P.I.V.O.T.™ becomes a simple reminder of what you already know, especially in moments when change feels heavy or disorienting.

If you remember nothing else, remember this: change is inevitable. How much additional struggle you carry through it is not.

I hope this book has helped you make change gentler.
I hope it has taught you how to **Dance With Change™**.

Acknowledgments

Dancing is never a solo act. Every step in this journey has been shaped by people who held the rhythm with me through encouragement, challenge, laughter, and grace.

First, to my children: you are my truest teachers. Your curiosity, patience, and courage remind me daily that growth doesn't come from perfection, but from presence. Thank you for allowing me to learn alongside you, and for grounding me in the everyday beauty of becoming—with humor.

To my mother and family, whose love, resilience, and faith laid the foundation for every chapter of my life. Even from oceans away, your belief in me has been the quiet pulse beneath this book.

To my friends and mentors around the world—across eight countries and countless transitions, thank you for helping me find belonging in motion and for anchoring me when I needed it most.

To my students and audiences—from classrooms to boardrooms, from Michigan to Gauteng and beyond, your stories, questions, and reflections brought this work to life. You reminded me that transformation is reciprocal: when I teach, I learn; when I lead, I follow; when I share, I grow.

To my early readers and supporters who offered critical insights woven into these pages— Ken Miller, Sara Feister, Rachael Tiesenga, Kolby Wasnick, Lisa Garcia, Beth Pappalardo, Jacob Cameron, Etienne Viljoen, Lisa Wexler, Alissa Nostas, Dean Whittaker, and Eric Mech— your feedback, encouragement, and belief in this work gave me the courage to keep writing on the hard days. Thank you for seeing yourselves in these pages and for reminding me that this work matters.

And to every reader holding this book now: thank you for saying yes to your own transformation. Whether you find yourself in the Pause, the Introspect, the Vector, the Overcome, or the Travel Forward, know this: you are not alone. We are all learning our way through the rhythm of change.

May we all keep dancing.

About the Author

www.dancewithchange.com

Dr. Khutso Madubanya is a global scholar-practitioner, author, change strategist, and transformational speaker who helps people navigate change with less fear and greater agency. Having lived and worked across eight countries and reinvented herself across a wide range of professional roles, she understands change not as a theory, but as a lived experience that reshapes identity, meaning, and direction.

She is the creator of the **P.I.V.O.T.™ Method**—a mental recalibration framework designed to help people build adaptability and ease as they move through disruption. Her work integrates research, real-world experience, and deeply human insight to support sustainable adaptation during transitions.

Dr. Khutso holds a Ph.D. in Business Management and has worked across academia, corporate leadership, public service, and the nonprofit sector. She is also the author of *No More Free Passes*, a reflective exploration of independence, identity, and the unseen cost of always being strong.

Through her **Dance With Change™** philosophy, Dr. Khutso equips individuals, leaders, and teams with the mindset tools to navigate complexity and transitions with clarity and empowerment.

www.ingramcontent.com/pod-product-compliance
Lightning Source LLC
Chambersburg PA
CBHW051541050726
47595CB00002B/585